DEEP FAITH,
Resilient Faith:

>>>—→

Curing Shallow Christianity

MELANIE J. SAWARD

Ark House Press
arkhousepress.com

© 2022 Melanie J. Saward

All rights reserved. Apart from any fair dealing for the purpose of study, research, criticism, or review, as permitted under the Copyright Act, no part may be reproduced by any process without written permission.

Unless otherwise stated, all Scriptures are taken from the New International Translation (Holy Bible. Copyright© 1996, 2004, 2007, 2013 by Tyndale House Foundation. Used by permission of Tyndale House Publishers Inc., Carol Stream, Illinois 60188. All rights reserved.)

Some names and identifying details have been changed to protect the privacy of individuals.

Cataloguing in Publication Data:
Title: Deep Faith, Resilient Faith: Curing Shallow Christianity
ISBN: 978-0-6455397-3-8 (pbk)
Subjects: Faith; Christian Living; Spiritual Growth;
Other Authors/Contributors: Saward, Melanie J.

Design by initiateagency.com

Contents

>>>>→

Acknowledgements v
Introduction vii

Chapter 1   Resilience in Faith 1

Part 1

Chapter 2   Unconditional Faith 20
Chapter 3   Seeking 35
Chapter 4   Waiting 51
Chapter 5   Freedom 71
Chapter 6   Community 89
Chapter 7   Managing Emotions 105
Chapter 8   Unconditional Love 120
Chapter 9   Jesus' Resilience 137

Part 2

Chapter 10   Obedience 150
Chapter 11   Service 158

Bibliography 167
Reflection Questions 169

Acknowledgements

As always, I must acknowledge Jesus Christ my Lord and Saviour who carried me on through this season of writing. Only you know how many distractions and trials threatened to take me off course this time. But by your grace, I have done this work that you have requested of me. I am honoured to share this message with your people.

To my husband Josh, who has listened to me as I lamented and grappled with the ideas in this book. You are so faithful, consistent and patient. Thank you for trusting me.

To my dearest Leela, who continues to grow into an incredible woman of God. I can't believe you are 9 years old! Thank you for being you, and helping me to stay young in my faith.

To my Mum & Dad, I will always honour the way in which you have brought me up. You have always kept life light-hearted, and amazingly somehow still deep and rich.

To Liz Swanson, for editing yet another book with finesse and grace. Thank you for pushing me in my writing skill, I believe it has been working.

To Pastor Paul & Pastor Pramila Jabez (and of course Jemima and Joseph too). Even though our relationship is new, I am still amazed at God's faithfulness to divinely appoint what has begun. I look forward to the years to come.

To my dear friend Lucy. For all the hours you have spent on the phone listening to me rant, hearing all the low points and the high points. What an incredible friend and confidante you are to me. Our friendship is one of the best things that came out of our time in Brisbane.

To my dear friend Hannah. We are finally in the same state again! Thank you for our incredible friendship that has lasted over 20 years. I always find compassion and hope when we share together.

And finally, to my dogs Buddy and Junior who have faithfully slept beside me snoring and whatnot during the long hours, and odd hours in my office typing away #workingfromhomelife #bestcompanionsever

Introduction

by Melanie Saward
15th October 2020

I could only just make out the purple flowers. It still wasn't clear to me what exactly I was looking at, but I was so drawn to it. I just had to get closer. Abandoning the path, I pursued this intriguing sight. As I approached it, the breadth of this vision came into full view. A stunning purple jacaranda tree. It was the central feature of the entire street. It perched prominently over the atmosphere, relegating every other object in its vicinity to background noise.

This dream came to me exactly seven months ago today. I hadn't thought much about that jacaranda tree until recently as I have found myself in one of the most difficult trials I have faced to date. As I pray and fast for a breakthrough, jacarandas keep popping up in the foreground of everyday life without me seeking them out. They remind me of that dream.

Yesterday, I opened my bedroom blinds and lay down. A glorious purple Jacaranda tree, standing in my neighbour's yard, filled the view from my window. I had never noticed it in the entire 6 years of living here. I came out of my first counselling appointment last week and sat in my car, only to look up and see the largest jacaranda tree I have ever seen. Another day I reluctantly went out to spend time with friends. I sat down at the restaurant, turned to my friend next to me and dangled above her…yep you guessed it: a jacaranda tree.

No doubt these jacaranda trees are a reminder that God is completely immersed in my immediate situation. Even more immersed than I was in the waters of baptism at 19 years of age. But God knows that this delightful vision represents so much more. It was an analogy that I had been pontificating about only a day before my dream.

Over the last few years, I have been forced to confront a very sobering reality; my shallow faith. It never occurred to me that my faith could be lacking, such was the arrogance I had. But I've realised that there are so many limitations I had that prevented the power and presence of God in my life, because of this shallow faith I had been living. If you were to ask my friends and family, they would probably disagree. I am often known to be that person who hears from God, earnestly, passionately seeks God and follows the leading of the Holy Spirit. But I know the bitter truth: I am shallow in my faith. My belief in God reaches as far as my rigid opinions begin. My grace is conditional; it depends on what they've done and my affinity for them. My obedience continues until my own political persuasions emerge. My willingness to give is reliant on my perception of my own personal wealth at the time. And I am often driven by my emotions and ruled by my thoughts. And if my circumstances were truly bad enough, I could probably give up on my faith and the body of Christ as I have previously contemplated.

And yet several years ago, as I really allowed myself to be consumed by the word of God, I realised that there was a vast difference between the faith I professed to live and the faith I read of in the early church. The early church wasn't perfect of course. And I am not attesting to some romanticised vision of the early church like we are sometimes guilty of doing. But when the rubber hit the road, the substance of my faith in 2018 was such

INTRODUCTION

that I was unlikely to sacrifice my life for the gospel. How could I have been? I couldn't even sacrifice my time, my possessions or my personal opinions. And I was a Pastor! The truth is, I'm probably not ready now to sacrifice my life for the gospel either. But if a life sacrificed were to be the measuring rod for commitment, I am making far more progress than I was several years ago.

Now some of you might be thinking I am being all too hard on myself. And you could be right. But this rant is not an opportunity to view any self-condemnation I may or may not have. And my agenda is not to project self-condemnation on the masses either. The main purpose of this rant is to recognise that the strength of our convictions in this modern world, seem to lack a real recognition of the power of this gospel that we ultimately benefit from. We have not grasped the depth of it. And I think it's because we don't nearly operate at the kind of depth in our everyday lives that is required to see it. We might be emotionally aware and be intellectually capable, but we don't know what it is to live with depth and drink from that well.

See, there was something about the nature of the faith that the New Testament believers in the Book of Acts had. They were committed fully to this gospel. Many of them sold their properties to share their wealth with the family of God. The widows were prioritised and cared for by other believers. They would live together and sacrifice their personal space. They met daily. They were able to perform mighty acts via the power of the Holy Spirit. And of course, they were persecuted and martyred. And yet they didn't have the biblical texts available for personal consumption as we do today. Their faith was demonstrated by their actions.

Comparatively today, we have more resources and opportunities than we could possibly imagine and yet a completely faithful life inspired by the gospel can still elude us. We have our Youversion Bible apps and personal reading plans and can connect to listen to the most insightful preachers anywhere at any time. We have copious amounts of professionally developed worship. We have pretty and inspiring posters available on mass. And a short visit to your local Christian bookstore will reveal a myriad of paraphernalia, from water bottles to mints encased with biblical precepts. We have thousands of churches across cities. We have more choice than the early church could have imagined. Most of us are ridiculously wealthy in comparison to the people of those days, and yet the substance of our faith is so hollow.

Don't feel bad. Once again, the intention here is not to condemn. It is to demonstrate one thing: the kind of faith needed right now is bigger than the one we have. The kind of faith we need is one that will last despite the greatest challenges thrown in its way. One that remains faithful and steadfast regardless of the season.

> *"But they delight in the law of the Lord,*
> *meditating on it day and night.*
> *They are like trees planted along the riverbank,*
> *bearing fruit each season.*
> *Their leaves never wither,*
> *and they prosper in all they do."*
> Psalm 1:2-3 NLT

It's generally not common for a tree to bear fruit in every season. But as believers, when we are planted in the right revelation when our roots have taken hold in good soil, it is possible to bear fruit in every season. Whether it is winter, summer, spring or fall. When the worst of each season throws itself at us, we can stay grounded...if the soil is good.

So, the jacaranda tree...

INTRODUCTION

The night before I had the dream, I was thinking about depth in our faith. I really felt like I was onto something significant. Because surely the depth of our faith has some level of determination on the longevity and steadfastness of that faith. I began thinking about the trees. I noted that for us to be like the tallest trees, we would need the deepest root systems. Only I discovered that the tallest trees don't necessarily have the deepest root systems, proportionately. The assumption I had held for decades turned out to be incorrect. The tallest tree in the world, an American Sequoia named General Sherman is up to 76 metres (250ft)[1] in height with a width of 9 metres (30ft) ...and yet the root system for the average Sequoia is only 3.5 to 4.4 metres (12-14ft) below the ground.[2] That is quite shallow when you think about it. It certainly made me wonder how it can even stay standing so well. On the other hand, the jacaranda tree might be significantly smaller standing at 10-15 metres high with a width of 10-15 metres[3]... but its root system is double the size of its width.[4] Looking around at our present society, both in and out of the church, many could be diagnosed with seeking the tallest spaces: prominence, status and beauty. And we are guilty of personal agendas, that would see us obtain those tall spaces. But these pursuits don't necessarily make for grounded individuals. We may not receive all the praise and glory amongst our peers for focusing on depth, but we would sustain an incredibly resilient faith, that is able to withstand any situation and make a greater impact in this world than any time before.

And as I sit here, continuing to contemplate the agony of my current trial...having cried out many times to the Lord in sheer desperation that immediate healing would take place...I note that this is not the path of

---

[1] Kiver & Harris (1999), 236
[2] Szalay (2017)
[3] Alpine Nurseries (2021)
[4] Chen

resilience. For whatever reason, in this season He would have me walk out my faith with patience and diligence with a confident hope that healing is to come at the timing He so desires. And I must continue. Because this is the path of resilience. See, resilience means that I can't simply run from this trial. Resilience means that I continue to dig down into the well of revelation that is not dependent on the nature of my circumstances. If I am truly pursuing the jacaranda kind of faith, I must choose to run toward the storm. Because it will create in me a resilient faith.

Please note: Unless otherwise noted, the English Standard Version (ESV) of scripture has been used throughout this text.

Chapter 1

Resilience in Faith

It is kind of strange to read the New Testament book of Thessalonians in which Paul is dealing with a bunch of Christians that have decided they need not do anything in life since Christ is returning soon. It was about 2000 years ago when that was written. We are now more than 2020 years post-Christ, and He still isn't here. Every generation seems to have its signs and predictions that suggest the time might be up, but nothing has ultimately happened yet.

Could we really be blamed for having complacency over the final days? It has been in excess of 738,000+ days since Christ. Surely, we can't maintain that level of urgency societally for two millennia.

Look, I don't know. There are those who declare that Christ is coming now, based on current world events. But despite what we discern about the times...God has directed us to be ready.

There are a few things that I dare say have worried me about the state of faith in the Body of Christ, including my own, and what we know about that day to come. Whilst many do believe COVID is a sign of the nearing end, the question of our readiness seems less of a discussion point. Matthew 24:9-10:

> *"Then you will be arrested, persecuted, and killed. You will be hated all over the world because you are my followers. And many will turn away from me and betray and hate each other."* NLT

Firstly, we are told that believers will be arrested, persecuted and killed. Many believers are experiencing this kind of treatment already. Around the globe, the persecuted church has been silently suffering for the gospel for decades. But for the average Christian in the Western world, this is not something we have ever really had to face. We certainly do not have the popularity that we once enjoyed. But it is still quite a gap in comprehension to imagine arrest, persecution and murder on account of our faith, compared to now.

Secondly, we are told that we will be hated. This is already partly true. Christians are not exactly a liked subset of the population. In fact, we are often interpreted to be the ones that hate, which God knows we are guilty of. Our response to this hatred depends on our own specific journey. In some cases, we have escaped so far into the Christian community that we don't have to associate with the outside world. In other cases, we try to argue and debate with those who oppose us, hoping that understanding might lessen their dislike of us. And in other cases, we try to soften the scriptures and focus on the aspects of faith that are more palatable. I don't know which response is right, but we certainly haven't always considered that the hate and rejection the world feels toward us collectively, may simply be a sign that we are getting closer to the day He returns.

Thirdly, we are told that many will turn away from Jesus. Yep, again already happening. Sadly, it is hard to tell whether the mass exodus of believers is a rejection of the not-so-modern church that is not necessarily moving with the needs of the next generation...or whether again this is a sign that Jesus is coming back soon.

And lastly, it tells us that believers will betray and hate each other. This is a sad state to contemplate since love was always supposed to be at the centre of the Christian community. Having written a book all about disillusionment, and journeyed with many people in that space, I can't even imagine what kind of brokenness this betrayal and hatred will create...or is creating. With such a future state approaching us, as Jesus described, we will require the protection, love and support of the Christian community more than ever. But instead, we may find betrayal and hatred.

Whatever the case may be, when we are called to be ready for His return, by default it implies that we are also ready for everything that will be thrown at us when His return is imminent. Whether that is hate, arrest, persecution, murder, betrayal from the Christian family and the temptation to hate each other.

All of this worries me though because I'm not sure we have the kind of depth in our faith as a Christian society in the Western world to handle all that we are told will come to pass. And this isn't some random verse that we can afford to ignore. It was spoken by Jesus. It is mentioned in three out of four books in the New Testament.

At this point right now, we are very attached to our lifestyle. And because we can pursue our faith in relative comfort (even with the changes COVID brought) we haven't had to consider whether we would stick to it were we in a life-threatening situation. And let's be real honest, some of us can't even handle being a little disliked, let alone rejected and hated as Jesus described. We are jumping through hoops, working real hard just to be accepted. By our Christian peers and our non-believing friends. Never to think that there may come a day when we will have to choose whom we are ultimately accepted by...our grey way of living will suddenly become painfully black and white, and not by our own choosing. Being hated to the point of arrest, persecution and murder is going to be really hard, and counterintuitive when our MO has been to keep people happy. Will our churches be able to handle this Un-life-giving message? Will they be able, to tell the truth even though it might change the number of people that turn up to church each week? Or will it be too late as believers who were convinced that Jesus should always build you up, walk away looking for a more positive message?

What will we do when feel-good Christianity is no longer relevant?

No one knows when He will return - but clearly mankind is not yet ready. I'm not ready, I declare as I sit in my comfortable chair with my big-screened Mac. And this is the time to be getting ready to have a faith that is deep enough and solid enough, that we will recognise the times we are in and endure it. Because who will turn and who will stay?

It is of utmost urgency that we become stronger and more resilient believers.

Resilience Level

Resilience has been studied to death. And I have no intention of extrapolating it further or adding anything to the already full body of work. We want to be stronger, to be able to cope with the many hardships in life and bounce back well.

But our faith and the depth of our convictions also have a resilience level. In a general sense, when we face something unexpected either faith in Jesus gets stronger and the relationship with Him gets deeper...or faith takes a hit. As much as we would all like to believe we would never give up on God, most of us do have limitations on what we are willing to endure for Christ. In the modern world where we are accustomed to the kind of self-help Christianity that tells us God intends for us to live a prosperous life...we are somehow able to believe that message, and still, accommodate the words of Paul. We don't even realise that we are reading the letters, standing on the words of someone whose values most likely opposed and confronted our present age. A man who would probably consider much of what we contend with, an utter distraction.

It is natural and normal for our faith to go through stages and changes, but if we are still continuing to follow the spiritual formation journey that God is continually leading us on, even with its ups and downs...we will end up with a better faith. A more resolute faith. A faith that loves God more than it did before. Which is more often than not, the crux of the matter.

So far this has been true for me, and I confidently assign credit to the ever-present grace that has carried me so obviously in recent times. In light of the painful disillusionment, I went through several years ago. And the severe potentially life-threatening phobia I went through in 2020. And the season of bordering panic attacks whilst I confronted my own sense of failure in 2021. While not painting a very great picture of myself, I am not ashamed because these three seasons were the catalyst for the kind of faith I deep down have always desired. The type of faith that nourishes my soul to such a degree that I might just be able to endure ANYTHING. The same difficulties that would have crucified my confidence 10 years ago have been the very things that have stared me in the face today. Yet, I do not fear as I once did: rejection, judgement, financial hardship, the fear of death, uncertainty, vulnerability...these are but a few of my recent companions. Initially, they were threats, now they are simply bystanders. All because

DEEP FAITH, RESILIENT FAITH

God revealed to me the priority of resilience in my faith. I am meant to go through hardships, not simply survive them...

When you have tasted the fruits of a resilient faith, no amount of oversaturated sugary prosperity gospel candy could compare. Having once espoused the values of a prosperity gospel without fully understanding it to be so, I never realised that there was an alternative. Until I was stripped of everything I once relied on to define my own personal prosperity. And what I discovered instead was that every trial is intended to grow us. Not confound our existing theology.

But of course, trials do confound the prosperity gospel because it demonstrates very quickly that victory is not the goal of faith. We are already victorious in Christ. Resilience is the goal. This is why Paul repeated over and over again: *'Stand firm'* (1 Cor 16:13, Eph 6:13). Because evidently, standing firm in our faith (not our opinions and doctrines, but the exercising of faith) is incredibly hard to do. Especially when the intention is to stand firm because of love and for love. There are many Christians standing firm today, in resistance to the surrounding moral differences. On the contrary, it is much easier to stand firm out of a sense of moral rightness. It is much harder to stand firm because you love God and love your neighbours. Especially when your neighbours resist you and everything you stand for.

Consequently, this is my renewed perspective: I'm not interested in having a prosperous faith that blesses me with external comforts and security. I'm interested in a resilient faith that can hold me steadfastly in the hands of God, even when I have no idea where I am going nor where my next paycheck will come from. I'm not pursuing prophetic words that inspire or encourage me, I'm pursuing an inner framework that doesn't need my emotions to be oriented a certain way to keep walking with Him: through the valley of the shadow of death or upon the clouds in glory. I'm not attracted to having a good life accompanied by creature comforts and wealth, but instead deepening my understanding of the nature of this good God who causes me to rejoice and wonder at even a moment's consideration of His goodness. I don't want to give my tithes and offerings as a selfishly motivated act for my own future surplus. I want to give my all, everything that is within me, good and bad to God as an offering, ensuring that no part of me is left inaccessible to His view and His moulding.

Because when you have a resilient faith, you don't even need some vague promise of prosperity. God is the only promise you desire to need.

A resilient faith in God is sufficient. And it is a better preparation for the coming times as Jesus described.

Firstly, let's debunk some myths and barriers.

Our Attachments

As always, I am preaching to myself. Having just moved interstate and now occupying a rented old house, versus our bought renovated one, I am again faced with my own hypocrisy. I want to live a life of complete abandon, where should God call me to Syria tomorrow I would have virtually nothing to pack because I have not amassed comforting material possessions. But instead, I have beautified our rooms in an effort to overshadow the peeling paint that makes me feel icky when I notice it. I loathe my middle-classness! I'm so mad at my parents for wanting to provide me with all those creature comforts they couldn't have! It's not their fault, I know. Such is the heart of every parent to give and provide a life without challenge and hardship.

Frustratingly we have NO IDEA. We don't think about how attached we are to this world and this life. Nor do we consider how much we pursue comfort. I am genuinely perplexed when I read the passage in scripture where Jesus releases the seventy-two disciples to go into different parts of Jerusalem. He essentially tells them, *'Take nothing with you'*. (Luke 10:4) My first instinct is: "What, not even a shaver? A toothbrush? Cleanser? How about a wide-tooth comb for my curly hair?"

We can't even relate to this idea, let alone all the other challenges that Jesus and scripture are often opening up to us. How about the fact that so many in the early church were selling their properties to pay for the believers? We just sold our house and ended up with a pretty penny and believe me this one hits home!

Okay, our preoccupation with material possessions is not completely ungrounded. Society has changed too, right? I am so grateful for the Australian superannuation scheme.[5] Because I'm pretty sure that my 8-year-old daughter is not going to house me and her dad when we are unable to provide for ourselves. Partly because her Indian grandmother has already called dibs! But also, because she will probably only be able to afford a 2-bedroom apartment in Sydney 20 years from now. She'll probably only be able to afford enough space for her future family. So, our attachment to such things may be because we can't so easily rely on anyone else to assure our future living status.

But material possessions are just the tip of the iceberg.

We are so attached to our lifestyles. Grabbing a latte from our favourite coffee shop on the way to work - which I have no intention of changing just because I wrote it here. Strolling through our neighbourhood markets to take in the atmosphere and vibrancy. Drinking a glass of wine on a Friday night with a few too many slices of Brie. God knows we deserve that creamy Brie. Having the six-monthly girls' getaway up the coast to rest and recuperate. The annual overseas holiday discovering the rustic alleyways of

---

[5] In Australia it is compulsory for Employers to pay 9.5% of your wage into a super fund which is accessible for you upon retirement.

Europe, fit for a postcard. Meeting a friend in the city to take in the latest musical or play.

It's no wonder we struggled with lockdown. For so many of us we have been reliant on our lifestyles to bring us joy, pleasure, relaxation and satisfaction.

This lifestyle is so ingrained into our being.

We are attached to our jobs, our careers and our sense of purpose. We often tell ourselves that we immerse ourselves in our careers and jobs to provide for our families. But so often we have opportunities to pay off our mortgages faster so that we could take jobs that are less demanding on our families...but we don't. We like the status our jobs give us, and the title we can drop at different social gatherings where we can quickly project to others what we want them to think of us. SUCCESS. IMPORTANCE. SIGNIFICANCE.

There is in part a tendency to fear and avoid death, because it reminds us that this life we have on earth will end. And we like this life we have on earth! We can't imagine that there might be blessings in heaven that would be greater than the bucket list of activities and experiences we've decided are the epitome of life. Yet there is so much of life to experience on earth. I still want to try pasta in Italy. Or see the Northern Lights. Climb mountains and all that jazz. But if we are more overcome with the treasures of this world than we are with the one to come, we surely do not fully understand what is to come. Or maybe we haven't had enough of a taste of the Kingdom life and the Saviour, to realise how good it will be. And we probably don't understand who this Jesus is, and this Holy Spirit in us. Because I'm sure we wouldn't crave for the things of this world, if we grasped it all.

For all of Jesus' earthly days, He never once ventured to a city simply to observe its beauty. Or to try its food. And He only lived for 33 years. The acknowledgement of His short life didn't cause Him to fit in as many experiences as He could. He didn't have an express bucket list. Because He wasn't attached to this life.

See our future, and the degree to which we can handle what is to come is hugely dependent on how committed we are to this earthly life. Our attachment to this life changes how eternally relevant our actions are. Revelations 12:11 states:

> "They triumphed over him by the blood of the Lamb and by the word of their testimony; they did not love their lives so much as to shrink from death." NIV

As a gunning Pentecostal, I had heard the first part of this verse thousands of times. Only recently I realised what this verse actually says. That critical to the equation of God's people overcoming the enemy, was the fact that they did not love their lives so much as to shrink from death.

The scriptures continue in this theme with the Apostle Paul making a staggering statement:

> "For to me, to live is Christ and to die is gain"
> Philippians 1:21 NIV

No, he wasn't suicidal. He wasn't depressed. He simply had a perspective of one who was not so attached to his life and all the goodness He could gain from it. He was more attached and connected to Christ than anything this life could offer Him.

In Luke 14:26 Jesus is recorded as saying, in one of the most confronting pieces of scriptures:

> *"If anyone comes to me and does not hate his own father and mother and wife and children and brothers and sisters, yes, and even his own life, he cannot be my disciple."*

At first sight, we might be confused. Is this Jesus speaking? Or the enemy? Okay, so Jesus isn't being literal when he says hate. He is saying that if we are more attached to our relationships here on earth, and even our own lives, we cannot be disciples. This is one of those verses that fly in the face of the mythical meek and mild Jesus.

> *"If your right eye causes you to sin, tear it out and throw it away. For it is better that you lose one of your members than that your whole body be thrown into hell."*
> Matthew 5:29-3

During my seasons of song writing, I have often wondered if blindness enhances song writing abilities. Afterall, there are musicians that are unable to see and they seem so much more connected with their sense of hearing. Apparently, there is scientific evidence to support this. In place of visual sensors, the brain rewires the other senses to be enhanced. Is this what Jesus means in the above passage? It would be better to be seemingly disadvantaged in this life with one working eye if it could advantage your faith. Just as the sense of hearing is advantaged, by the loss of sight. There is *nothing* more important than our faith and relationship with Jesus.

There is plenty in scripture that displays clearly what it looks like to have a life that is detached from the pleasures and comforts of this world. And often our journey toward a resilient faith is one that seeks to disconnect those things that we have depended on for the kind of satisfaction that only God and the richness of His kingdom could provide.

The weight of it all...

Based on historical events, Paul is thought to have been beheaded. Peter was apparently crucified upside down. James the son of Zebedee was most likely executed. Andrew was said to be crucified. Thomas supposedly pierced with spears. Matthew was stabbed to death. Simon the zealot was apparently killed after refusing to sacrifice to the sun god. And Matthias who replaced Judah is said to have died by burning.

Besides demonstrating the myriad of gruesome deaths available on hand in that era, the martyrdom of our spiritual ancestors speaks to us a critical truth. They declare something that our positive modern church cultures are too scared to insinuate: this gospel is worth dying for. The value of the Gospel is so great that life itself is worth sacrificing.

Have you had a look in the mirror lately? Have you reflected on who you are? Because you may see Tom, Jane, Nick or Sophie. A face that you have been staring at for all of your life. But according to scripture, you are a dynamic testimony of Christ. Somewhere along the way, we have been distracted. We started to believe that our doctrines, our churches, our conferences, our morals and values, and a blessed life were the greatest testimony of Christ to this world. Yes, all these things may tell a portion of the story of Christ's goodness. But the word says that WE are the vehicle through which Christ touches this world. We are the demonstration of His incomparable grace. We are His living testimony. What happens in us, our ability to endure, our ability to live out the fruit of the Spirit in the face of hardship...this is the testimony of Christ, the gospel and His goodness.

When we give up on Christ in any form, whether it is a whole or partial[6] rejection of His involvement, we make a bold detrimental statement:

"This faith is not worth it"

But when we persist through anything this world throws at us, uncompromising in our desire to know Jesus, resisting the temptation to be angry, to blame, to judge, slander, spread false witness and covet, we declare something in our actions that our mouths will never have to verbalise:

"This faith is worth everything"

We also attest to the value of Christ and the gospel, by how we live. Are we willing to abide, even when our vision of Him is blurred amidst hardship? Are we willing to keep walking alongside Him, even when He takes us in a direction we don't like? Is this faith enough of a revelation that truly nothing could deter us from being fully consumed by Him? Even if we were never to gain in this life for our faith, would we still follow Him?

The truth of the Kingdom-way is that we die before we truly live. We crucify the flesh, we put to death the old life, we take up our cross. We die now, so that we can live forever.

All that must die in us for the sake of Christ, cannot be done without a faith that can handle it. A resilient faith is the only kind of faith. No other kind will do.

---

[6] We call ourselves Christians, but we really aren't living a life where we believe that Jesus is all we need.

PART 1

Introduction to Part 1

It has become customary for all my books to have a section that is dedicated to understanding the signs that would indicate a certain state. For instance, in my book about Disillusionment, I spent time exploring what it looks like and what kind of behaviours would present if you were disillusioned. In the chapter about Pride in 'Ministry Stinks,' all the signs that you might be struggling with pride are listed. I do this because:

1. The heart is illusive
   Jeremiah was wise when He stated:

   "The heart is deceitful above all things, and desperately sick; who can understand it?"
   Jeremiah 17:9

   We want to believe the best of ourselves, but the heart is not easily understood. Our intentions are not easily understood. Our agendas are not easily understood. We might say that we want to do good, but often just a few trials would have us acknowledging that our goals were self-absorbed and focused on self-glorification. And why would we expect anything different, when Jeremiah also reminds us that our hearts are sick. Or to use a more modern and accepted term, our hearts are broken. Our hearts can't expect to be anything but deceitful, because they receive and perceive through a very broken lens. This is how it is indeed possible to commit sins and crimes, and all sorts of behaviours all the while assuming it is everybody else's fault.

So, when I ask someone what their intentions are, when it comes to some action they are about to take, I am confident that a proportion of their response may be influenced by not only what they want me to hear...but what they want to hear. And I apply the same degree of sober judgement of myself. I don't just assume that what I feel, or think is true of my situation.

2. Our behaviours are a better representation of our beliefs

I can tell myself anything. I can express whatever I desire to project to everybody else. But I can't fool my behaviour as it will only express what is true in the deepest parts of me. For instance, I often tell myself that I want to be a healthy person. And it's at least true in my intentions. But when push comes to shove, I have some pretty established unhealthy habits. So, the truth is, I want to be a healthy person up until it impedes my desire to eat what I want. So, do I really want to be a healthy person? Probably not as much as I tell myself. Thank God I am a work in progress and at least willing to confront what I see, rather than what I tell myself. There is probably a greater chance of conquering my poor habits this way. In this day and age, we are obsessed with what we want to project about ourselves. We say we love all colours and creeds, but we are blind to our own prejudices. We say we care about injustices when we march down the streets, but we don't necessarily give to the poor. I don't want to be like this, but I know I am. And I assume you don't want to be like this either. So, the only way to change is to face the hypocrisy in ourselves. To see what is true,

INTRODUCTION TO PART 1

and not just what I want to say of myself. In 1 Peter 1, the Apostle Peter has just been commending the people of God to live a holy life, when he says in 1 Peter 2:1:

> *"So put away all malice and all deceit and hypocrisy and envy and all slander."*

Peter places 'hypocrisy' in the company of deceit and malice. I don't know if we would technically class hypocrisy as sin, but we certainly wouldn't assume that it belongs among such strong words. And it's strange that we have deceived ourselves in this way, since Jesus frequently spoke against the hypocrisy of the Pharisees and Sadducees.

If we are truly to be obedient to Christ, we ought to shed every ounce of pride that would prevent us from dealing with our own hypocrisy as Peter encourages here.

And to that end, we must consider what we do...the truest expression of what we believe.

I write all of this to warn you that this next section will be a deep excavation of resilience. Each chapter will be an extrapolation of a core foundational pillar in the journey toward a truly resilient faith. Take time to consider if these words, represent how you live in relation to God and others. To face the inconsistencies, that you might have a steadfast faith in Jesus alone.

Chapter 2

Unconditional Faith

Whenever I read the story of Jacob, I find myself annoyed. How could God have favoured this man who sowed deceit everywhere He went? I feel the pain of Esau's cry when He asks His Father for a blessing. And I shake my head at what appears to be a lustful desire for Rachel. If I am allowed to say such things, I don't like Jacob much as a Biblical character. The only saving grace is where He wrestles with God. But admittedly it's the God who is willing to wrestle that I am enticed by.

The truth is, we have more in common with Jacob than we would care to admit. We may not necessarily go out and intentionally deceive those around us, but we certainly get what we don't deserve. We certainly have favour in spite of our sinfulness. We receive blessings like a firstborn, even though Jesus had to sacrifice Himself for us to have it. And of course, we have all fought many times in our lives for self-sufficiency in order to gain what God has mercifully promised.

There is much we can learn from Jacob, particularly in Genesis 28.

Jacob has a dream. He dreams of a ladder that connects earth with heaven, with angels that descend and ascend upon the ladder. It's a famous dream often referred to as 'Jacob's Ladder'. During this dream, God makes this incredible covenant with Jacob:

> *"I am the Lord, the God of Abraham your father and the God of Isaac. The land on which you lie **I will give to you and to your offspring**. Your offspring shall be like the dust of the earth, and you shall spread abroad to the west and to the east and to the north and to the south, and in you and your offspring shall all the families of the earth be blessed. Behold, **I am with you and will keep you wherever you go**, and will bring you back to this land. For **I will not leave you until I have done what I have promised you.**"*
> Genesis 28:13-15

God makes a covenant with Jacob. He promises the land to Jacob. He promises offspring. He promises blessings. And He promises that He will not leave Jacob until He has delivered on all He has said. This is a big deal. It's an unconditional covenant. Which means that it is not based on what Jacob does. Jacob is unable to forfeit this covenant through stupidity or sinfulness.

It is difficult for us to comprehend the unconditional nature of a covenant. The fact that God makes a commitment to anyone despite how they behave is ludicrous. What could He possibly have to gain? Can you imagine making a commitment to someone else that would not be affected or changed by their treatment of you? Or their treatment of others? This is a level of faithfulness that we just cannot comprehend. Almost all relationships we have here on earth are conditional, whether or not it was meant to be that way. When we sign a contract for a new job, we agree that we will maintain employment up until the conditions of that contract are unmet. When we make friends, we conditionally agree to support and love each other until one person, or another fails to meet the expectations of the other. When we purchase a product from an electronics store, we are exchanging money with the condition that what they have advertised is accurate. And even marriage, although a covenantal relationship, has the condition that each party is faithful, and should infidelity arise the other is able to divorce (although this is not unanimously endorsed by all believers).

So many laws and contracts exist to govern these agreements we make, to ensure that the conditions are not unfairly weighted. But at the end of the day, a conditional covenant is one that allows clauses for both parties to abandon the agreement should certain situations come to pass. This was not the nature of what God was giving to Jacob.

Now not all covenants that God makes are unconditional. The Promised Land and the inhabitation of that land by the Israelite people was a conditional covenant. Therefore, they didn't continue to live in the Promised Land.

But you wouldn't think that God would make too many unconditional covenants, considering how little experience we humans have with them. You'd think that the first time an unconditional covenant ended with an unfaithful partnership, the occurrence of such covenants would cease. And I'd be the first to stand up and say "Amen Lord! Why should you get the raw end of the deal?! Protect yourself oh Holy One". The point is, no one would blame Him at all if He were to give up on making unconditional covenants.

But what would our response be to such a commitment made by God to us, like that of Jacob? Would we freak out? Afterall it is a little overwhelming. Would we worship Him? Would we fall on our knees and weep at the loving nature of God?

Well, I can tell you what Jacob did. He worshipped. He declared "How awesome is this place!" And the next morning He built an altar and named the place, Bethel. After doing all of this, He made a vow:

> *"If God will be with me and will keep me in this way that I go, and will give me bread to eat and clothing to wear, so that I come again to my father's house in peace, then the Lord shall be my God, and this stone, which I have set up for a pillar, shall be God's house. And of all that you give me I will give a full tenth to you."*
> Genesis 28:20-22

Now I appreciate Jacob's honesty. But at the crux of this vow, is this very important word: 'if'. Jacob has just been given this incredible promise by God. An unbreakable vow that essentially has nothing to do with whether Jacob deserves the promise. And His response after doing the rituals, is to respond with a conditional covenant. Now the truth is, He didn't have to make any covenant in response to God. In fact, He could be commended for doing more than was necessary. Here's the mind-blowing fact about an unconditional covenant: it doesn't obligate the person to respond or counteract with a subsequent promise or vow. God doesn't make unconditional covenants because He is looking for another way to get us to make a commitment to Him. No doubt it is likely to produce desires in us to respond. But it certainly isn't made with the expectation that the individual will respond in the same fashion. So it wouldn't be fair to think harshly about Jacob. Especially not when the truth is that we generally don't respond any better. Unlike Jacob, we aren't really aware that we are making a conditional response. Which creates problems of its own.

What we observe in Jacob mirrors many of our lives when it comes to our faith that:

> *A conditional response indicates a transactional relationship.*

When we have relationships that are conditionally oriented it means that we have put certain clauses, even if unstated, on the nature of that relationship. We may have subconsciously asserted that there is a transactional nature underpinning the relationship. As long as both parties remain partially satisfied that those conditions are being met, we remain faithful.

That's what Jacob was saying. As long as God delivered on these promises, He would continue to live and worship Him.

I have seen many people walk away from the faith. And surely, I also have come painfully close to walking away too. The worst part of this process is realising that there were conditions in our relationship with God that we didn't know existed. Whether He gave us a spouse, or that our children would be believers, or that our church is our family or the career accolades and promotions that we thought He wanted too.

And sadly, because we are often avoiding trials or simply complaining our way through them, we miss the opportunity to see the substance of our faith. Or more specifically the conditions we have subconsciously attached to that faith, that create a conditional framework for God to operate within.

God is often trying to remove these conditions! Part of His transformational process involves living for Him...not our conditions. Intimacy is really difficult to achieve in a transactional relationship. By crying out to

God to feel His presence and His love, there is no acknowledging the massive plank that skews our vision of Him.

The truth is, the difficult and painful truth that we must confront and confess is: we are often only one or two 'unmet-conditions' away, from it all falling apart.

What could a conditional faith be telling us?

At the time of receiving this unconditional covenant from God, Jacob had not been through a great deal. His story had been marked by two events only, in which He was the main perpetrator deceiving his family members for personal gain. It was the challenges he experienced after with Laban that might have humbled him. His uncle deceptively coaxed him into double the length of tenure by deliberately giving him the wrong wife (she was not the 'wrong' wife since the lineage of Jesus came from her offspring). And as you read the narrative of Jacob, it is possible to see a change in Him. A kind of pre-Laban and post-Laban state. And of course, Jacob has His wrestle with God which may just be the climax and culmination of the years of hardship under Laban, and his deceptive past catching up with him.

There are a few possibilities as to why Jacob might have responded to God with a conditional promise, and by shedding some light on this we may also be able to understand our own tendency to respond with a conditional faith:

- **He didn't comprehend the significance of the covenant**
  The covenant made with Jacob had been previously made with his grandfather and consequently his father. He may have known of the promise made to his ancestors, but it's possible that something was missing in his own comprehension of this promise. Maybe he

didn't understand that this was not a promise that God made to everyone. Or that this promise was actually unconditional. We are often guilty of such comprehension issues. We might frequently hear that God loves us, and yet we still expect to find punishment when we come to Him in our darkest times. Therefore, phrases like "Jesus loves you", can make little difference to some believers. Because the statement relies on the listener having an accurate understanding of who Jesus really is, and that they comprehend the idea of love as it is defined in scripture.

- **His relationship with God was in its early phases**

    This may not have been the first time God appeared on the scene in the life of Jacob, but it was the first time he would be able to recall personally. The first time God showed up was at his birth when he told his mother that *"the older shall serve the younger"* (Genesis 25:23). So, it is fair to say that even though Jacob would have known of God, there isn't much to demonstrate the depth of his own relationship with God. And of course, the same can be the case with us. Certainly at the beginning stages of my relationship with God, I didn't have the history with Him to experientially comprehend just how faithful He is. I believed that God was present in my difficult time. But I didn't understand how my freedom would be found when I laid it all down, good and bad for Him.

- **He was selfishly ambitious**

    When Jacob takes his brother Esau's blessing, He is guided by his mother. He even has reservations about how easily they can pull off the deception (Gen 27:11-12). So, it's possible for us to place some of the responsibility upon his mother. But earlier when he trades food for Esau's birthright (Genesis 25), Jacob acted completely alone. His brother may not have been so famished that he was going to die, but Jacob saw the situation as an opportunity to gain something for himself. Not a time to display brotherly love. This is an example of selfish ambition, when the drive to work hard and advance is motivated by selfish gain. This is not a trait that we are encouraged to have. In fact, Paul states in Philippians 2 that we are to do NOTHING out of selfish ambition. For this reason, Jacob may have interpreted even the unconditional covenant that God gives him through the filter of selfish ambition. His words are quite interesting:

"If God will be with me and will **keep me in this way that I go***"*

Jacob apparently knows where he is going, and the value of God's promise is seen in God's ability to keep him in this 'way that He is going'. He is viewing this promise through the lens of how it will enhance and advantage the path He has determined to walk on.

We don't see the similarities between ourselves and Jacob when we read the stories of deception, but it is commonplace for us to view God for what we can gain from Him. It is considered normal to view God as our supernatural sub, that comes in temporarily to improve the game of football that we are trying to win.

The crux is that a conditional response to His unconditional love tells us that Jesus is probably not our Lord. The conditions are our Lord. It tells us that we probably don't love God as much as we think. And maybe most importantly, we don't really think God is as good as we perceive Him to be, to keep walking out this faith. Because as scripture reminds us, it is the goodness of God that leads us toward repentance.

Everyone has their weaknesses. Everyone is tempted. For me, it was becoming successful. I worked myself, often to my own detriment, with the intention to kick goals. My resume became one long list of achievements that I battled to grow. There was no situation that couldn't be strategized through, and there was no job that I couldn't conquer. I had a 10-year plan, and I was going to get there. Whilst I still sought God and followed the Holy Spirit when it came to which job I applied for, I valued myself most when I was achieving my goals. It wasn't until I found myself in a season where nothing seemed to move me forward, that I hit rock bottom. And realised that all my efforts to achieve goals were formed from this deep need for significance. I had been chasing success to feel important. It didn't get better initially. I just continued to see how difficult it was to love and serve God when my conditions weren't being met. How difficult it is to have good character, to be grateful and content when I didn't see the favour, I wanted for the goals I had devised. Ultimately, I wanted to quit His plan for my life...

But my commitment to depth made me pause and consider that this might have been my 'conditions'. The conditions that I hadn't acknowledged, sat between God and me and the glorious relationship I could experience with Him.

Counting the Cost

In Luke 14:26-33, Jesus is describing what it takes to be a disciple.

> *"If anyone comes to me and does not hate father and mother, wife and children, brothers and sisters - yes, even their own life*

- such a person cannot be my disciple. And whoever does not carry their cross and follow me cannot be my disciple.

"Suppose one of you wants to build a tower. Won't you first sit down and estimate the cost to see if you have enough money to complete it? For if you lay the foundation and are not able to finish it, everyone who sees it will ridicule you, saying, 'This person began to build and wasn't able to finish.'

"Or suppose a king is about to go to war against another king. Won't he first sit down and consider whether he is able with ten thousand men to oppose the one coming against him with twenty thousand? If he is not able, he will send a delegation while the other is still a long way off and will ask for terms of peace. In the same way, those of you who do not give up everything you have cannot be my disciples." NIV

Jesus is proposing the conditions that are required if we are to be disciples. He addresses the relationship we have with our parents, our children, our siblings...and even the value we place on our own lives. He is saying in an expansive way, that our commitment to being a disciple must be without condition. We must be willing to forego it all, even life itself, if we are to be His disciples. Therefore, He is encouraging His listeners to consider the high cost. Though it's not any higher than what He was willing to do Himself.

Being a disciple, according to Jesus, is to have an unconditional faith. A commitment to follow Him wherever He leads. Even if that commitment means you will be rejected. Even if that means that you lose your name and reputation. Even if that means you will lose your life.

This couldn't be a more radical idea.

Would we give everything up right now, to follow Jesus? Unconditionally? No matter what we stood to gain or lose for it?

Unconditional Faith is a precommitment

I have a practice that I do from time to time. Some might find it morbid, but I consider it critical in the pursuit of resilient faith.

The practice is, asking myself a question: Would I be willing to give this up? Whether I am talking with my daughter or writing a great podcast... would I be willing to let go of this?

Here is another angle:

Would I still follow Him if…?

You may not want to know how extreme the situations are that I envisage filling in those blanks, because it may be confronting for you. But here are just a few:

- If my husband left me
- If I ended up poor on the street
- If God called me to the most dangerous country in the world to evangelise
- If a book I wrote didn't sell a single copy
- If I never had another child
- If I had to endure torture

Whether they happen or not, is not nearly as important as my answer to the theoretical synopses. I proactively search for these hypothetical scenarios because I want to know what subconscious conditions I might have so that I can plough through them with God's strength and have an unconditional faith. You might think this is crazy! But the kind of faith that makes us strong, is the faith that has no conditions.

So many believers would say yes if they were asked, would you die for your faith? But the truth is, we are being asked by Jesus to die to ourselves every day. Sometimes that is the harder question to say yes to. If we aren't willing to die to ourselves every day, to our agenda, our comforts, our lifestyle, our opinions, our money...why would we expect to answer yes when the day comes to lay our physical body down? How many opportunities do we reject not realising that it was our 'die to ourselves' moment for that day? We resist healing through therapy because we are too scared and uncomfortable with the pain we will experience in the process. When that might have been our die to ourselves moment. We avoid the smaller church because the bigger church is more fun and has better facilities and services. But that might have been our die to ourselves moment. A pastor might use 'submission' theology to get a volunteer to do as they say. But that might have also been their 'die to ourselves' moment. Biting your tongue. Picking up the dish. Forgiving the person who hurt you. Sending a gift. Inviting someone in. Treating your troublesome child kindly. Providing a roof over someone's head. Intervening for the oppressed. Reading the Word. Surrendering the desire to be right. This might all be our 'die to ourselves' moments. And God invites us every day to humble ourselves, by dying to ourselves.

The fact is, to have an unconditional faith we are essentially making a precommitment. It's not waiting until you are in an awful situation to decide whether you will follow Him. It is making a commitment prior to the circumstance arising that you will follow Him. It is knowing that there are no 'if's' because you have declared it. Maybe raising hypothetical scenarios may help you decide if that is something you can do. But either way, a precommitment is the best preparation for the challenges that will no doubt come.

How does a precommitment change how we live out faith?

See there is something that changes in us when we decide to make a precommitment that we will follow Him no matter what:

> *We know that we MUST get through all challenges brought before us.*

Trials are no longer these situations that are undesirable and unwanted. They aren't optional. They become an expectation. Because we realise that nothing poses a greater growth opportunity than a trial. We could read our Bibles every day, pray three times a day, go to church three times on a Sunday and we will still not stand to grow as exponentially as what hardship could do in us. A trial may be the literal solution to a subconscious faith condition that we didn't know we had. And every trial becomes a time of building for a future that we may not be able to handle in our current faith-state.

Nothing has prepared me more for the possibility of being rejected by the Christian world...than being rejected by my church leadership. It was still devastatingly unpleasant at the time to be rejected by people I loved and trusted, but when I received a text message from a stranger recently who had seen a post and proceeded to accuse me of being the antichrist, I was able to not crumble into metaphorical ash. I had developed the resilience to handle that kind of rejection. The kind that comes from a brother or sister in Christ.

A precommitment encourages us to see through a situation. Because the situation is no longer the threat. The real threat is not learning. Or not deepening. God is the only one who can discern the hearts and minds of His people. He knows what conditions we have. And He knows what crutches we must let go of, if we are ever to become a true disciple and receive all that true discipleship promises to bestow.

Not a perfect faith

It would be negligent of me to fail to state this next point. Because every religiously led person, with perfectionist tendencies may not see this truth.

God is not asking us to have a perfect faith. He is not saying that we are to go through every trial without complaint, pain, lamenting, frustration, support and friendship.

It's okay to need a counsellor. It's okay to need a small group. It's okay to ugly cry for as long as you need. God is not uncomfortable with tears, and He doesn't get tired of them.

It doesn't even mean that He is against you having questions. Having an unconditional faith is to endure all with a deep conviction of who He is and that He is your companion through all situations. The fact is, God always intends for us to change our selfishness in the process of a trial. If you walk away from a trial more angry, more judgemental, more hurt there's a good chance you missed the point. All hardship leads to more love. For God, and for people. Our love for God is meant to grow, because it is the love that makes us willing to have an unconditional faith.

> *"This is how love is made complete among us so that we will have confidence on the day of judgement: In this world we are like Jesus."*
> *1 John 4:17 NIV*

In the first part of this verse, we are reminded that the love we have in us is not made complete and that the intention is that it would grow. Our love is imperfect. And we therefore participate with God's journey of forming us in order to grow the love in us.

God is not looking to us for perfection. It's the willingness to keep following Him. It doesn't matter what kind of mess you are in as you walk out His will for your life. You will have scars. But they will be healed if you walk the path with humility, ever ready to hear Him speak and direct you, as you follow. Scars ensure that we never forget. He is there for you and will carry you through. Make the precommitment that you will endure and stand firm in your faith in Jesus.

The Truth

Many of us may not be able to make that precommitment. And that is okay. Honesty is much more effective in this process of counting the cost, than unfounded bravado and arrogance. I know what my difficult conditions are because of my hypothetical scenarios. But what I do say to God as I walk through these imaginary scenarios, knowing well that I don't right now have the resilience for such a situation…is that I will walk through anything if He is with me. And I know He is with me. Whatever I don't have the courage for now, I trust that His love will prepare me for in my coming days. And so we ought to take every opportunity to learn and grow. We eat up every trial knowing that it equips us for the unconditional faith required to be a true disciple of Jesus Christ.

Chapter 3

Seeking

My Indian mother once told me, "Mel, Indian people don't get divorced". Although that isn't entirely true, I understood what she was trying to say. Even when Indian people have unhappy marriages, they will often stay together. I've seen it time and time again in my extended family, family friends and many more. In 2019, India was ranked as having the lowest divorce rate in the world at 1%. Consider this in contrast to the USA's divorce rate at 44%, the United Kingdom's divorce rate at 42% and Australia's divorce rate at 38%.[7] Additionally, the couple recorded to have had the longest marriage, a whopping 90 years, was an Indian couple: Karam and Kartari Chand of Bradford, UK (Karam died at 110 in 2016 and Kartari died at 107 in 2019).

So, I guess my mother was right, although I don't think she knew how statistically accurate her gross generalisation was.

Of course, the length of a marriage doesn't indicate health, a fact frequently noted when discussions of marriage statistics in India arise. But at

---

[7] Nguyen (2022)

least for Karam and Kartari, they demonstrated every sign of being happily married for their 90 years together.

The question that every enduring married couple inevitably asks when they meet a couple that has been married for more than 25 years is:

What does it take to stay married?

Truth be told, most of us may not even live to 90 years, let alone be married for 90 years. But I'm sure you can imagine that this is not at all a new question. Plenty of studies have been done to find out what secret ingredients provide the framework for a long happy marriage. Communication is regularly referred to in such discussions. As well as love. Commitment.

Besides the specific verses that pertain to marriage, the Bible also speaks of a marriage that will amazingly exceed Karam and Karturi's 90 years: the great eternal marriage between Christ and His people. The marriage of the bridegroom and the bride. In Revelations 19:6-8 an angel is showing John the celebration to come when Jesus returns for His bride:

> ""*Hallelujah!*
> *For the Lord our God*
> *the Almighty reigns.*
> *Let us rejoice and exult*
> *and give him the glory,*
> *for the marriage of the Lamb has come,*
> *and his Bride has made herself ready;*
> *it was granted her to clothe herself*
> *with fine linen, bright and pure"—*
> *for the fine linen is the righteous deeds of the saints."*

SEEKING

As the bride, we are in the season in which we are preparing ourselves for the marriage that is to come. This marriage is so different from Karam and Kartari, or any marriage you and I could experience on this earth.

Our challenge will not be whether we remain in union with Christ after the wedding day. The test for those of us who believe is whether we will remain faithful in the preparation. Whether we will indeed remain a part of this collective called the bride. And this is not as simple as it would seem. Jesus reminds us that not everyone who shows the signs of being a believer, will enter the Kingdom of Heaven.

> *"Not everyone who says to me, 'Lord, Lord,' will enter the kingdom of heaven, but the one who does the will of my Father who is in heaven. On that day many will say to me, 'Lord, Lord, did we not prophesy in your name, and cast out demons in your name, and do many mighty works in your name?' And then will I declare to them, 'I never knew you; depart from me, you workers of lawlessness."*
> Matthew 7:21-23

Even those who prophesy, who heal, who drive out demons and other mighty works, may not enter. We often presume that a person capable of healing or performing mighty works is highly anointed. A deeply spiritual person. But this passage reminds us that such mighty works are not necessarily the sign of obedience. Nor is it a sign of preparation.

What does all of this tell us about remaining in faith until the day of the great marriage? It tells us that it is critical to understand how to 'stay in love' with the bridegroom.

****

Recently a prominent leader asked an intriguing question on an Instagram post. "How do you stay passionate for God?"

Passion is an interesting word. Passion is attractive. It's engaging. It's motivating. And I've heard a lot of sermons about it. But the scriptures don't really tell us that God requires us to have passion as we often define passion. What scriptures do tell us, is that we are to love the Lord our God with all our heart, mind and soul. And that may or may not look like passion. A better question might be: "How do you stay in love with Jesus?"

Naturally, such questions will attract the classic Sunday school responses:

- Read the Word
- Spend time with Jesus
- Worship

Yes, they are rather cliche. But the truth is, we are kind of at a loss as to how to answer this question. It's actually not easy to answer without the cliches. And up until a few years ago, I myself really didn't have anything better to add besides the cliches.

Part of the reason our response falls short is because this question isn't really designed to get a 'what' answer. It's not really a list of specific activities to undertake that draw you into a loving relationship with Christ. Although that may be a starting point. The difference between whether we come to love God, or whether our activities become a routine, is what we desire whilst we do those activities. The difference is whether we are 'seeking' Him.

'Seeking' is a term that is used frequently throughout scriptures. Furthermore, it is a multi-dimensional word. There are about 10 Hebrew words and 6 Greek words that are frequently translated into 'seek' in our English translations.

SEEKING

I didn't realise the value of this word until only a few years ago. Before that I understood this word in one light: to pursue God's opinion on a matter. Usually by way of reading scripture. Which of course is true. But with 16 dimensions to this one word, it would be impossible for this definition to be all that is intended by the word.

There are plenty of verses with the word 'seek' commonly referenced in the Christian community. Here are a few significant ones.

The word for seek, ***Zeteo*** (Greek) means to intentionally pursue, desire or strive after.

- **Matthew 6:33**
  *But **seek** first the kingdom of God and his righteousness, and all these things will be added to you.*

- **Matthew 7:7**
  *Ask, and it will be given to you; **seek**, and you will find; knock, and it will be opened to you.*

- **Luke 17:33**
  *Whoever **seeks** to preserve his life will lose it, but whoever loses his life will keep it.*

The word ***Daras*** (Hebrew) often translated as seek also means to enquire, to search, to investigate, to ask for. It may mean through prayer and supplication, or study.

- **Deuteronomy 4:29 CSB**
  *But from there, you will search for the Lord your God, and you will find him when you **seek** him with all your heart and all your soul.*

- **Jeremiah 29:13**
  *You will **seek** me and find me, when you seek me with all your heart.*

Baqas (Hebrew) the word translated can mean to demand, to seek with the intention of finding.

- **Psalm 27:4**
  *One thing have I asked of the Lord, that will I **seek** after: that I may dwell in the house of the Lord all the days of my life, to gaze upon the beauty of the Lord and to inquire in his temple.*

- **2 Chronicles 7:14**
  *If my people who are called by my name humble themselves, and pray and **seek** my face and turn from their wicked ways, then I will hear from heaven and will forgive their sin and heal their land.*

It may seem as though there are only subtle differences between these words, but in all three cases the word is a verb. Therefore, in order to apply the concept of 'seeking' the subtleties become more significant in action. Just like the colours aqua, turquoise and teal. In theory, distinguishing these three colours for the average person would not necessarily make a great deal of difference. But in the design or art world, understanding and recognising the subtleties between them is critical to one's success or failure, particularly once the paint hits the canvas.

So, it may be simple enough to identify God's opinion of sin by perusing scripture. But how do we search for God as Jeremiah 29:13 mentioned earlier implores us?

SEEKING

You will seek me and find me, when you seek me with all your heart. Jeremiah 29:13

This is not referring to a search for His opinion, or guidance. This is talking about finding God. Which is directed at the Israelites who already knew God. Or to us, who have already found Him. See there is a distinction between His personhood and nature, and His opinions. Though they are so closely related. One requires vulnerability and the other is largely an intellectual pursuit. I have met many children who can recite extensively the opinions their parents hold, but they know little about their feelings and personal experiences. They know how their parents like their tea, their favourite colour, which political party they vote for, who they hate, who they love, vaccinated or unvaccinated and every other opinion that we could possibly have. But they know little about how their parents felt when they missed a job opportunity. Or what they desire most for their kids. Or the depth of love they have for their spouse. The point is, it's possible to know every Christian principle and doctrine, but not genuinely know the Father. Or His love. Or how He feels about you specifically.

When we read the word 'seek' and consider all its dimensions, we see that God is suggesting an activity that is robust, involving and all consuming. We cannot simply seek Him by completing a task or a daily habit. It's a pursuit that requires the intensity of someone we would label obsessed or fanatical.

There is more

There is an underlying presupposition inherent in the task of seeking, as the scriptures describe 'seeking'. To seek means there is more to find. To seek, presumes that there is infinitely more to God than we are currently convinced we can see. To seek God like this means we are convinced that we have not arrived at a full knowledge of who He is.

Now most of us would agree in principle to this fact. But for so many believers, they by no means behave as though this is true. They live as though there is nothing more to find in God. As though they have arrived at all there is to know.

How can you tell this?

There are a few signs of a believer who has given up the search for God:

- They've stopped reading their Bible, praying or participating in any other spiritual discipline. Only the bare minimum may be done, such as going to church.
- Or if they do still read scripture, even if it is every day, they only notice what affirms their existing beliefs.
- Their prayers are a list of wants and rarely do they ask for God to show them more of Him.
- They are unable to be vulnerable with God. Their prayers are declarations, instead of conversations detailing their fears and hurts.

On the flip side, a believer who engages in a deep search for God will do the following:

- They will read scripture expecting to see things that they haven't seen before. They frequently speak of their shock at this counter-cultural text.
- They pray desperate prayers.
- They are frequently working on things about which God is speaking to them.

- They are quite okay with not knowing all the answers to their questions.
- They know they still have lots to learn

When Job, who lived faithfully for God, faced the classic conundrum of suffering, God obliterated His preconceived ideas by His response. God details the acts He has done and the incredible knowledge He has of life and this earth, to remind him of who He is and who Job is in retrospect. He says things like:

> "Where were you when I laid the foundation of the earth?
> Tell me, if you have understanding.
> Who determined its measurements—surely you know!"
> Job 38:4-5

Job and his friends were sitting, trying to allocate blame for the suffering he had experienced, assuming that they judged the situation with all the knowledge that could possibly exist. At the end of God's gargantuan soliloquy, Job responds:

> "Therefore I have uttered what I did not understand, things too wonderful for me, which I did not know."
> Job 42:3

Besides all that Job teaches us about wisdom and suffering, it also gives us this lesson. That God is way too wonderful for us to comprehend, and that wherever we are in life and our relationship with Him, we are only perceiving Him according to what we know AT THAT TIME. The purpose of seeking is to find God. And the God we find the first time we meet Him, is not necessarily the enormity of God as He really is. It's just the facets of God that we are most capable of perceiving at that point in time. Therefore, our goal is to have an ever-growing revelation of God. It should never stop. I'm not talking about knowledge accumulation, although sometimes that can help. But it's primarily a relational revelation.

Sometimes the reason we get stale in our relationship with Christ, or we fall away, is because the vision we have of Him has not changed. And anything that lives, that gives life, must grow and improve. Even if it is just our perception. And in this case, our perception of this God we love.

Shallow Research and Drawing Near

Sometimes I will use the word 'research' fairly loosely. I have classified a Google search as 'research'. Okay, definitely not often. And certainly not for my books.

But Google is an amazing source. I have learnt how to do a lot of things because of something I Googled. But sometimes it does perplex me when I consider that most of us might dedicate 10-20 minutes 'researching' a topic that our intellectual ancestors may have dedicated 40 years to examining. In fact, I feel a little guilty about that.

Unfortunately, the ease in which we can obtain information influences our ability to seek. We aren't used to having to dig so deep and persistently to find something we are looking for.

> *"Draw near to God, and he will draw near to you."*
> *James 4:8*

Even though God loves us so dearly, and we receive the Spirit of God from the moment we are saved, God still loves to be pursued. He doesn't reveal everything about Himself to every person who wants to know. He leaves it in our hands to decide the degree to which we want to draw near to Him. So right now, whatever you know personally about God is likely to be the degree to which you have wanted to know Him.

There are barriers to finding God in our existing Christian practices. The ones that I had been taught and relied on all my Christian life. As much as I had devoted my life to Christ, I had done so because it was the right thing to do. I knew what I saw in scripture to be the right way to live. But I couldn't really be sure that I loved Him, although I was unwilling to voice that reality. The truth is, even though I had heard people say a billion times that God loved me, I knew I didn't feel that love. I had been reading my Bible and praying for decades. I'd faithfully follow the S.O.A.P method. Have you heard of the S.O.A.P method? It's an acronym that stands for:

S = Scripture
O = Observation
A = Application
P = Prayer

The idea is that you read scripture, you note anything that sticks out to you and consider what is going on and then you ask yourself how you can apply what you've learnt. The only problem is I had heard preachers and teachers say that the Bible is the revelation of who God is. The priority of scripture is that it tells us who Christ is. Even in the Old Testament the stories are a foreshadowing of Christ. The lamb that was provided to Abraham in place of His own son. Boaz as the Kinsman-redeemer. Esther who intercedes with the king on behalf of the Jewish people. And of course, many more stories pave the way for the coming of Jesus.

So, what I couldn't work out after decades of using this method, was why we had taken a God-centric text, and inserted a person-centric application?

I had lived my Christian faith long enough to know that if we can really change ourselves through self-awareness, we probably had some personal benefit to gain from it. Yes, that's right. We are unable to change on our own. That's one of the critical components of faith, for which we need a saviour. Here's the thing: you can grow without God. People do it every day. But they do it for some kind of personal gain. It's not out of the purity of surrender to a loving Father. Even Christians, their motivation to change is not necessarily to become like Jesus…it's to be a better parent, or leader, or feel more righteous. Hence why preachers must resort to messages with a 'what's in it for me' undertones. Because some teaching no longer inspires change.

> *"And we all, with unveiled face, beholding the glory of the Lord, are being transformed into the same image from one degree of glory to another. For this comes from the Lord who is the Spirit."*
> 2 Corinthians 3:18

The statement *'beholding the glory of the Lord'* could also be *'reflect the glory of the Lord'* (NLT). Other translations state *'beholding as in a mirror'* (NKJV), whilst still others state *'beholding as in a glass the glory of the Lord'* (KJV). This passage most likely refers to Moses and the time He spent face to face with God, when scriptures tell us that Moses' interaction with God made His face radiant.

> *"When Aaron and all the Israelites saw Moses, his face was radiant, and they were afraid to come near him"*
> Exodus 34:30 NIV

One translation says that the *'skin of His face shone'*. It implies that rays of light were emanating from his face. This is a pretty intense transformation! Not only is the description shocking, but the Israelites and Aarons response is indicative of how alarming this sight must have been.

The underlying concept in 2 Corinthians 3:18 is that what we actually see of God, not what we think we see is what has the power to change us. Transformation is a natural by-product of a true vision of God. The problem is that when we do a person-centred application, it's not God we are seeing. It's ourselves. So, all we need to do to change, is to see God as He really is. But how can we do that, if we aren't really looking for Him?

On a practical note, I have stopped asking "How can I apply this?" when I read scripture. I've started asking "What does this show me about God?" "What does it demonstrate about who He is?" This single change in reflective questioning has revolutionised my relationship with God. I'm not trying to change myself. I'm trying to change what I see.

The Mystery of God

It doesn't take most people long to discover that I have a special kind of love for my father. My dad is incredibly wise, very approachable and listens intently. He is always kind, always gentle to the point that it shocks people when he gets angry or upset.

As a child I adored my dad. I didn't just love him, I respected him. And not because the Bible told me to. In fact, I didn't need anyone to tell me to love and honour him. My respect was out of a response to the goodness I saw in him.

So, as I have grown older and he has shared more with me about his upbringing, and life experience, I have come to love and respect him even more than the one-dimensional father I saw as a child. He had his own challenges, hardships, trauma, and responsibility. He is a human being, who once was a son, who is a brother, a musician, a student. I see many more dimensions in him than I did as a child. And of course, I have seen him in his latest dimension as a grandfather.

The same can be said of God. When we first begin a relationship with God, it can feel strange to relate to someone we haven't seen before. But with time, a picture of God begins to form in our mind. With continued intimacy our picture of God grows. We begin to see Him in a multitude of dimensions. Father. Saviour. Friend. Creator. And so on. But for many of us, just as with our own parents, we grow up. We get busy building our lives, tending to our responsibilities. Even if we touch base with our parents daily, our objective isn't to learn more about who they are. We do it to make sure they are okay and update them on the kids.

When we were children, we talked to our parents with wide-eyed wonderment at their funny and amusing stories. I see this with my 9-year-old nephew, who adores his father, my brother. Whenever he is over at my house, he asks me a million questions about what his father was like when we were kids. He listens with excitement and anticipation, wanting to discover more. My daughter is the same. One day she came home upset telling me that a kid had been picking on her. To help her not feel alone, I told her about the time a kid picked on me at school. She was enthralled. Her response was part-shock, part-awe. She wanted to know everything about the situation. But I could tell by the questions that her greatest interest was in me. The category of 'Mum' in her brain was expanding to include this new dimension that she hadn't known before.

Oftentimes the longer we are believers, the less awe we can have for God. We hear the same old messages and the same old calls to action. And unfortunately, it can all become a bit routine. Before we know it, the touching base prayer we do to God each day is an obligatory act. Something you do because you think you should. Or because it's just something you've always done. Seldom does your communication have an underlying desire of discovery. Even if you are grateful. And even if you do love Him.

There are so many dimensions to God. It's possible that even though we have had scripture for thousands of years, that we still don't comprehend certain aspects of God. Furthermore, a knowledge of God does not mean we know Him and His attributes personally. The Pharisees and Sadducees were experts of the law, and yet they couldn't recognise God in the flesh. They knew about God, but they didn't know God enough that He would be familiar to them when He finally arrived. What a terrible tragedy.

The scriptures make known God's wondrous nature repeatedly:

- **Psalm 86:10**
  *For you are great and do **wondrous** things; you alone are God.*

- **Psalm 105:5**
  *Remember the **wondrous** works that he has done, his miracles, and the judgments he uttered.*

- **Psalm 136:4**
  *..to him who alone does great **wonders**, for his steadfast love endures forever.*

Even God himself tells Habakkuk, recorded in chapter 1 verse 5:

*"Look among the nations, and see; **wonder and be astounded**. For I am doing a work in your days that you would not believe if told."*

The adventure of discovering God, doesn't end in our lifetime. There will NOT come a day in which we will be unable to ask, "Who is God?" And there will never be a day where there will not be a new answer to this question. Or a new light to shed on an existing answer. He is capable of such never ending inspiration for those who seek Him with ALL their heart.

The fact is when we seek God, we are in essence attempting to discover more of the mystery.

If you want to stay in love with God, you must seek Him with the conviction that there is still so much more to be known. And He will reveal Himself to you. And when you see who He truly is, and your image of Him continues to be refined, you will come to love Him more and transformation will be inevitable. If you are still relying on one revelation you had 20 years ago to fuel your faith, there's a good chance your faith is dry! Our resilience in faith relies on a growing revelation of who Christ is. It relies on the multiplication of wonder and awe. And that is why resilience relies on seeking and why it relies on revelation. Because love grows the more you know. And the more you see. Love grows through revelation.

Chapter 4

>>>→

Waiting

"Then the Lord said to Abram, "Know for certain that your offspring will be sojourners in a land that is not theirs and will be servants there, and they will be afflicted for four hundred years."

Genesis 15:13 (above) is the first time God mentions the coming slavery of the Israelite people at the hands of the Egyptians. The generation of Isaac and Jacob was yet to pass before these 400 years of bondage would eventuate. But God speaks to this period of oppression two generations before, perhaps in a way acknowledging the severity and preparing the Hebrews.

Fast forward to Egypt. Jacob had passed and so had Joseph before a Pharaoh with no attachment to the past began to oppress the growing population of Israelites. And thus began 400 years of foretold slavery, with all its terror.

There are so many difficult questions this narrative of scripture raises. But you certainly would struggle to miss this one: why did God wait 400 years before intervening? Oddly enough, this 400-year time frame appears again in scripture. Between the last prophet of the Old Testament and the coming of Jesus, there were 400 years of silence. Again why 400 years? Why is this such a significant number?

There are some who believe that the number 400 holds some symbolism. But it is really difficult to ever be truly certain of that. What all believers would agree on, is that 400 years is a really, really long time to wait. And even though we know that God is sovereign, given the authority we would probably jump at reducing such a sentence. And it's this kind of fact that leave atheists and haters to question the compassion and righteousness of God.

Waiting is rarely tolerated or enjoyed. It is possibly the one area where we truly and so obviously diverge from the divine. Because whilst we seem to vehemently dislike waiting, God seems to enact seasons of waiting quite freely for His people. I've never met a single person who has said they like waiting, and that they receive it with joy and gladness. Waiting, for the average Christian is an interruption. A barrier. An unnecessary evil.

We have all had to wait for something: healing, the salvation of a loved one, job opportunities. And sadly, we all will. The experience seems so universal that you would forgive my cynicism at prophets that frequently prophecy breakthroughs for those who are waiting. I must silence that voice in my head that wants to remark 'well that's a safe prophecy!" because there is always at least a handful of believers that are waiting for something, and in some cases many things to come to pass.

I can't imagine a more frustrating topic than waiting. Even for those who surround the one who waits. From the minister to the faithful friend, we don't know quite what to advise for a person who is in a season of

WAITING

waiting. I've heard messages from the pulpit that condemn and judge the person who decides to wait for something. It's seen as laziness or a lack of service. No doubt there are times when a Christian is hiding behind waiting as though it were a godly endeavour when really, they are simply a habitual procrastinator. At least with Jonah, He didn't wait in his hometown remarking "well, I just want another confirmation from God to assure me that He really wants me to go to Nineveh". No, he ran in the opposite direction. I think sometimes we'd prefer to hear that. Our getting-things-done attitude would rather hear someone being intentionally disobedient than someone who is passively disobedient and parading it as holiness and wisdom. Sometimes.

We inevitably provide solutions for our friends geared toward escaping the season of waiting. We are simply not aware of it. Our struggle to advise and support a person in waiting reflects our own frustration and puzzlement at why waiting is necessary. We don't really know why anyone must wait. We logically might have some ideas: God is preparing us, God is preparing the right circumstances, He has our good in mind...But deep down, we just don't know what God is doing when He makes us wait, especially when the waiting is so torturous and painful. I don't know what to say to my friends who At 40 years of age have wanted nothing more than to have children, more than I ever did, and they are still waiting for a godly husband. I don't know what to say to my friends who have endured physical illness, praying and believing for a miracle, and it still has not come to pass. All of this confounds our theology about God, how truly loving He is and how faithful He is...but we rarely think to consider that the issue might be our theology of waiting.

Some General Things We Must Confront

In the Christian world, we often want to see great acts of faith. We are inspired and encouraged when we hear the story of Elijah who commands fires from the heavens and proves His God before the Canaanites. We love the story of Peter healing the blind man. We rejoice with David when he slays the giant. These are courageous acts of faith that we desire to emulate in our own life. But we often fail to honour the faith that is required to endure a season of waiting, and how favourably God looks upon such things. Romans 4:3 discusses the faith of Abraham.

> *"Abraham believed God, and it was counted to him as righteousness."*

Because of Abraham's faith to believe that he would have a son, a promise that we estimate he waited 25 years to see, God considered him righteous. A critical factor in the faith of Abraham is the fact that he waited and did not lose faith. Not just the miracle of birth in old age. We may dislike waiting, but it is our opportunity to demonstrate God's faithfulness in a way that is undeniable. How else could a 100-year-old man and a 90-year-old woman conceive and give birth? It is both a testimony to God's miraculous power AND His faithfulness.

There is no greater crucible in this world than waiting and suffering. Especially when combined. Change is assured where waiting and suffering persist. Maturation is a given. Yes, it can go either way. You can become an angrier and more bitter person. But you also can grow to be a more loving and patient person. We have a choice over how well we fare in the season of waiting.

And for that reason, there is no dilly-dallying around this fact, and the reason we must include such a discussion in this book: Waiting builds resilience. When done correctly. If we want to become resilient believers who are able to handle everything that could be thrown at us, waiting must become a tool rather than a curse.

Why must we wait?

The most common question during a season of waiting is "why?" Why must we wait? If we know a certain outcome is nigh, besides the suffering produced by waiting, what could possibly be so critical about waiting? I have waited at length for many answers to prayer, and I can't always say that I understand or visibly see the benefits. We know the Holy Spirit can act swiftly and promptly, so why then does God require us to sit in uncomfortable, even threatening situations when He has the power to act? There are many reasons that this might happen, which we will explore in this next section.

Waiting forces you to let go

By nature, we aren't great at letting things go. In fact, we are quite the opposite. Letting go is often a painful process. Letting go of a desire that we pursue can be followed by years of disappointment. Letting go of an unhealthy relationship often takes a significant amount of time processing the hurt.

We tend to want to own and possess and that can leave us at a loss when we are made to release our grasp, particularly when it is beyond our control. But letting go is a critical factor in our journey of faith.

Part of the problem is that in these modern times, we have far greater control than we acknowledge, particularly in comparison to our brothers and sisters in Christ in developing nations or even our spiritual ancestors. The seasons no longer have complete control over the kind of food we can eat. We can have strawberries and avocados whenever we want. We are not confined to the area in which we were born, we can pursue adventures in other states and even beyond our own country. If the water doesn't taste great through the tap, we can simply buy our own water.

We have become so accustomed to this level of control over everyday factors in the First World, that once upon a time, would have crippled nations i.e. lack of food, inability to move/migrate and unsanitary water. It was a miraculous thing that God gave foresight of the coming famine through the Pharaohs' dream and Joseph's interpretation. It was unheard of that Ruth and Naomi travelled by themselves to return to Naomi's homeland. And it was opportunistic to embark on a relocation to the Egyptian nation, due to their blessed water supply. These days we don't relocate for better water and plentiful food. We move for love, for better pay or just because we don't like the lifestyle of a relatively comfortable city. We don't move out of necessity, we move for personal satisfaction.

But if everything were in our control, why would we ever have to wait? The truth is we are not in control of a lot of factors. The journey toward maturity in many ways is the process by which we learn to discern the difference between what we can control and what we cannot. There is no other circumstance quite like waiting to remind us of that.

One of the greatest ways a season of waiting demands that we practise letting go is by reminding us that at least for a season nothing can be done. And indeed, sometimes nothing is meant to be done. If arriving at some destination wholly and solely relied on us and the actions we could do, in what way would we be relying on God? How would we ever observe His faithfulness? How would it be His will coming to pass? The objective of every believer, different to those outside of this Kingdom system, is following God's will. A concept that requires the involvement of God. We are often so busy trying to activate the critical components that would have us succeed toward our goal, that we won't consider the intricate factors that must and can only be achieved by God.

Waiting changes our perspective

Sometimes when we are so focused on our vision, we never stop to consider whether this vision is actually from God. Or at least whether He is as obsessed with it as we are. Because sadly, our reasons for seeking something are not always wholesome. There are times when my desire to play a particular role or position has come from the brokenness that I was trying to fill in my own strength. I am grateful for the years that I worked in church ministry, but I must confess that as much as I did love the people I led, there were times when my desire to lead and to advance positionally were because I wanted to fill some lifelong desire for significance. I believed that if I held a position that would mean I would have to be heard. That I would be a somebody, and not a nobody like I usually felt. It would finally mean that I was important.

I never stopped to question the deeper needs that motivated my pursuit. It wasn't until I stopped working in church ministry, and began my journey as a stay-at-home writer, that I was made to confront these feelings, because of waiting.

In this position of waiting, God was able to start dealing with the deeper unseen issues. And I am a different person for it. I no longer perceive ministry this way. The waiting was significant in reorienting my perspectives.

During a season of waiting, we desperately want the circumstances we are in to change, but it is us that needs to change. It may not be that the goal must change, but maybe we need to do it for a different reason than the one we thought. We can often be selfish in wanting to arrive at these destinations, not realising that for most of us these God-given future visions given us are primarily others-focused. That doesn't mean we won't enjoy that future, but our callings and our ministry are for the extension of His Kingdom, or for the edification of the Body of Christ. Which means that it's not necessarily for our pure enjoyment.

These are the kinds of perspectives that may need to change, that waiting can bring to the surface. And we can't be others-focused until we understand why we perceive our calling as an opportunity for us to gain. And furthermore, be willing to lay that calling down for the benefit of our neighbour and ultimately God's glory.

Waiting teaches us the truth about time

So much leadership literature these days is about trying to achieve more in less time. Time is precious, and we want more of it so that we can achieve everything that we want to. But the harsh reality about time is that we don't own it. We can't possess it. If it could be possessed, it would have already glided through our hands with the next passing second. Because time is always in motion. As are seasons.

God OWNS time. He will decide when the earth has existed for its intended purpose. He will decide when all of this must come to an end. And because He has oversight of all that must come to pass for earth's days, He also knows the right timing for all things.

Generally, our struggle with waiting is our battle with impatience. We want things to happen when we want them to. And then as believers, we try to deny our frustrations by reminding ourselves that "God's timing is perfect". The truth is, we often don't think His timing is perfect. This is why we lament and distress. We really don't like His timing. But this happens because we judge His timing within the context of our plan. If we were to consider His timing according to His plan, we might agree with this ancient truth.

Waiting is necessary so that we have a healthy concept of time. The truth our modern attitude avoids is that there is no need to rush the will of God. In fact, our rushing probably makes little to no impact on the timing of His will besides frustrating us. All that must come to pass, will never be of greater importance than having a sweet and pure spirit. This is why rushing is such a deadly compromise. We rush around thinking we are doing God a favour, but all we really are doing is compromising our character and priorities for His will to come to pass, which is on His watch…not ours.

Waiting builds character

Suppose I was to ask you this question: If we could all have what we wanted when we wanted it…what could happen? What impact would it have on our society? What impact would it have on us? There are already people in this world that believe they should have what they want when they want it. We often refer to them as rapists, burglars, drug lords and gamblers. There are the lesser condemned too: manipulators, extreme control freaks and liars. The fact is that so much of the sin that is echoed throughout this world is because someone believed that they should be able to have what they want when they want it. And the consequences to society are devastating.

The point is that if we didn't have to wait for things, we would never wait. And the less we have to wait, the more accustomed we get to not waiting. And when your ability to wait is so underdeveloped and your desire so intense, when the opportunity arises for you to have what you want with the potential of an adverse impact on someone else, you won't even think twice about it. Such is the way so many end up hurt.

Scriptures tell us time and again that endurance builds character. There are two key ways waiting improves character:

1. **Waiting forces us to become less invested in preferred circumstances**

    Daydreaming can show us a lot about ourselves. Fantasies, frequently our imagination's most self-centred musings, that we formulate in that time of daydreaming are often our preferred circumstances. The things we'd really like, that are subconsciously motivating our actions. The fallacy about these daydreams is that they presume without question that circumstances could genuinely please us. But if we are discontent enough to escape to the realm of fantasy, the problem may not be the circumstances and rather how we are interpreting both our situations and our theology. One of the most significant reasons those in the Early Church were able to contemplate death for the gospel, is because they understood that by the power of the Holy Spirit and the future coming of Christ, they had far more to gain than any preferable circumstance could give them here on earth.

    It doesn't take long to work out that generally the rich aren't happy. And the poor aren't necessarily any happier either. And don't even get me started on the middle class. So clearly our financial status is not a lasting or reliable determination of happiness.

    The beautiful and famous aren't necessarily any happier either. And neither are the forgotten and physically undesirable. Happiness is not determined by any status in life.

If we lean into the voice of scripture, we are told that such attributes like peace and joy, these rich words from which contentment and satisfaction find their place are a product of the Holy Spirit (Galatians 5:22). They are not experiences that are reliant on our circumstances to ascertain. Theoretically, we could for three years, not go anywhere, not see anyone, not have any money, not achieve a single thing and yet still find peace and joy as a gift of the Holy Spirit.

2. **Waiting causes us to value that which we have had to wait for**

I have observed the parents who have a child they have waited for, prayed for, cried in anticipation of…and the expression of love they have for their child is special. They don't necessarily love their child more than other parents, it's just that their perspective is unique. They really understand what it means when the Bible says that a child is a gift from God. Because waiting causes us to really value that which we have waited for. Like the single mum who has patiently and consistently saved her dollars, that might have felt meagre in the beginning, but now has the money to buy an apartment. She doesn't see just an apartment. You watch her decorate that home like it was a mansion. Because she values that which she had to wait and work hard for. We may think that we really want something, but how patiently are we willing to wait to have it? That is the test of value. If we are really convinced that it is worth it, we will wait. And all who benefit from us arriving at the desired provision, whether it be a career, a ministry, a child, a husband/wife, will be grateful for how the waiting formed the weightiness we now give that provision.

The fact is we become fixated on the destination. The goal-oriented, outcome-obsessed culture we exist in finds it hard to value the journey. But the journey is often more significant than the destination because the destination isn't what changes us. The journey does.

The journey is the act of faith. The journey is the place where all the hard work is done. It's where the real gold that the scripture talks about is found: a transformed heart.

Waiting proves God's faithfulness

What we believe about God is put to the test when we are forced to wait. We face the strength of our convictions, particularly our beliefs about God's love for us. Often we think that if God loves us, He ought to intervene and end our suffering. And that would seem fair at the time. But scriptures tell us that:

> *"Because the Lord disciplines those he loves, as a father the son he delights in."*
> Proverbs 3:12 NIV

What an unfortunate matter that this word 'discipline' has often come to mean a harsh reprimand. The ultimate purpose of all 'discipline' is to teach. According to scripture, the fact that God cares enough to teach us, guide us and lead us is the very expression of His love. Our society doesn't necessarily agree with this. Our society would rather have a god that has no comment on their actions and choices. But if you really think about it, inattentiveness is the opposite of genuine love and care. If we were to develop a scale of 'care' to determine what is considered the most caring parents, zero would be those who are completely uninvolved, unaware and uninterested in their children. In episode 2 (season 12) of Law & Order SVU, there is a young girl around seven years old who had been terribly neglected, due to her parent's addiction to video games. She appeared shabby and neglected and was leaving the apartment to venture through the dangerous streets of New York City to source her own needs. Most of us would agree that this is considered zero on the care scale. Even her basic needs that she was unable to provide for herself, were left unmet. This is the epitome of NOT caring. To act as though a child doesn't even exist is as good as not existing.

God is not at all like this. He cares intimately and holistically for us and all humankind. Even if we don't like what He has to say we can't deny that He cares.

Thus, making us wait may be His expression of care to us, that we might not rush in with carelessness. It is when we wait that we allow God an opportunity to demonstrate His faithfulness to us and others. Does not Joseph's story continue to remind us of God's faithfulness to His word? Despite every injustice that Joseph experienced, he remained the victor because God did not forget what was prophesied in his dream 13 years before. The very dream that caused his brothers to cast him aside. And yet within this narrative, God's faithfulness is also demonstrated to the people of Israel and Egypt, and even Joseph's sinful jealous brothers. It was God's providence for the famine that would surely have wiped them out had He not enacted His will through Joseph's life.

If we want to see the faithfulness of God, sometimes we need to step aside and allow Him the room to be our God.

And the final reason we must wait is that waiting is the only action that can grow our ability to wait. There is no other muscle we could develop to improve at waiting, than the act of waiting itself. And we need to be able to wait because Isaiah tells us that it is *'they who wait for the Lord shall renew their strength'* (Isaiah 40:31).

God's Waiting

There is no being in this universe, in the existence of all time and space, that has waited more or longer than God Himself. Thousands of years had supposedly passed between Adam's sin and the establishment of the first covenant. And now we are in the period of waiting until His second coming, which again has taken thousands of years. God's plan has not been a sudden, impulsive, panicked emergency rescue. It has been a long, exhaustive, global, steady plan of full-scale redemption.

He patiently waits for each generation to accomplish His will. He patiently waits for each person, often for an entire lifespan to turn toward Him. He is not simply driven by the overall outcome. He is committed to the journey with us both individually and collectively. However long it takes.

And so, we return to this earlier question: why did God wait so long? Why did He wait around 400 years to lift the enslavement of His people under this nefarious Egyptian regime?

To answer this, we must expand the parameters of the passage previously referred to:

> *Then the Lord said to Abram, "Know for certain that your offspring will be sojourners in a land that is not theirs and will be servants there, and they will be afflicted for four hundred years. But I will bring judgement on the nation that they serve, and afterward they shall come out with great possessions. As for you, you shall go to your fathers in peace; you shall be buried in a good old age. And they shall come back here in the fourth generation, for the iniquity of the Amorites is not yet complete."*
> *Genesis 15:13-16*

WAITING

The best reason theologians can find for the length of time the Israelites spent in Egypt is because the Amorites, inhabitants of the promised land, weren't ready. They were sinful people with perverse practices. But as God suggests in verse 16, their sin had not reached the level to which His compassion was ready to expire. In other words, He was giving them adequate time to repent.

Why did Jesus entertain the presence of a Jezebel in the church of Thyatira recorded in Revelations 2? The best answer we have, in His terms is because:

"I gave her time to repent..." (verse 21)

Why has it taken so long for Jesus to return? Again, the best answer is found in 2 Peter 3:9-

"The Lord is not slow to fulfil his promise as some count slowness, but is patient toward you, not wishing that any should perish, but that all should reach repentance."

Time and again, God's primary motivation is compassion and mercy. Just as it was when He sent His Son to the cross to be the solution to our sinful nature. He is painstakingly patient, beyond our comprehension, beyond our comfort level, all because He desires to give humankind as much time and opportunity as possible to be restored to Him.

This is true for our own seasons of waiting also. We rarely consider this, but maybe the reason we must wait is not even for ourselves. There are plenty of promises that God has given me that I am still waiting for. I used to lament often over these promises, but once I realised the reasons God waits, I couldn't complain anymore. Maybe the reason I must wait for my promises is that their untimely delivery would have an adverse effect on my daughter and her own salvation story? Maybe it might negatively affect my marriage? Maybe the promise itself is a little less about my own personal fulfilment, and a lot more about the salvation and discipleship of many? Would I be more patient than to ensure that these circumstances were just right so that God could maximise His redemption story for others? I believe I can. This life is not about me. And it's not about you. I. We are valuable, we are important. But this universe doesn't centre around the accomplishment of my goals. This universe centres around God's all-encompassing, detailed plan to redeem this world. We can all wait a bit more, whilst He accomplishes His plan. Is it possible that we have not contemplated the depths of His great compassion and mercy if we thought He would ever rush? Do we realise how much we have benefited from His patience? I became a Christian at eight years of age, but it took 10 years before I had a real relationship with Him. And it took another 20 years to really comprehend the need to surrender my will for His sake! We must wait, so that our future brothers and sisters in Christ may benefit from His patience too.

Now here's the part that can have us giving up: sometimes we are suffering as we wait for God to extend mercy to others. In the case of the Israelites, they were harshly oppressed for hundreds of years because God was giving the Amorites a chance to repent. How do we reconcile this? How do we understand that we endure suffering at the hand of God's mercy toward others? Where is His mercy for us in our suffering?

Well firstly, it is not right for us to assume that the oppression of the Israelites was only because of the Amorites. God also had plans to accomplish in Egypt. We have read about him informing Abraham in Genesis 15. God had a plan for the Egyptians too, that He was accomplishing through the Israelites.

Secondly, this should again cause us to consider the depths of God's mercy and compassion that He would wait so long for a nation to repent, before giving up. We can understand this better when we consider the love passage in 1 Corinthians 13, which primarily describes the perfect love of God. Specifically, it describes love as *'always hoping'*. His patience is so long because He continues to believe the best of His creation. He believes that despite all humankind's sin and consequential devastation to this world, repentance is not so far away. It's not so impossible. He believes that the Amorites can change, and so He gives them an adequate opportunity with plenty of warning before consequences are enacted and prophecies of destruction come to pass.

But thirdly, and maybe most importantly for our question, we must understand that in our suffering there is always this promise: that God will heal and restore those who have hurt or lost. He promises to always be our comforter. To always be our friend and companion through the times of suffering. He often carries us through such seasons, displaying His kindness and faithfulness. According to scripture, whilst such times are hard and difficult, He guarantees us that if we remain faithful in those times that our reward is greater character and understanding of God.

His love and comfort have no end. It will always be available to us. But the opportunity for redemption is limited. Even when it comes to salvation, we only have this time now to accept His invitation. Through my book 'Disillusionment', I have naturally acquainted myself with people that have gone through different traumatic situations, including spiritual abuse. It is crazy to me when I think of how long a narcissistic minister may stay in his seat of authority when those around them are suffering. I used to cry out to God. But then I realised that God gives them a chance to repent, often for longer than we are comfortable with because when He executes the consequences of their disobedience there will be no turning back. Love, comfort and healing are always available. But the opportunity for redemption is limited.

Hope

What we cannot afford to ignore is that there is a relationship between waiting and hope in scripture. We don't simply wait because it is a necessity. Waiting is not baseless and without a deeply rooted theology. Biblical waiting is not done without hope. We are told in Proverbs that

> *"Hope deferred makes the heart sick"*
> *Proverbs 13:12*

This is a reminder that whilst we are waiting for something to come to pass, the greatest threat will be to our hope. It is our hope that deteriorates first in a season of waiting. And yet hope is the very concept we hold onto when we endure. We have a hope that God is who He says He is. That He will honour His word. That He will provide a pathway for delivery. These are the convictions we put our hope in.

So why then do we still feel 'sick' as the Proverb suggests?

Isaiah 40:31 may give us some insight:

> *"But they that wait upon the LORD shall renew their strength; they shall mount up with wings as eagles; they shall run, and not be weary, and they shall walk, and not faint." KJV*

I have read and pondered over this verse countless times, particularly as I have waited eagerly to see Gods will come to pass in my own life. This verse tells us that in our waiting we ought not to feel 'sick' but rather our strength shall be renewed, we won't tire or be forced to give up. But the truth is, this is the opposite of how I have often felt during my seasons of waiting. So how could this be? How could our experience be so contrary to His truth?

The secret is in the phrase *"wait upon the Lord"*. In this instance, the word used for 'wait' in Hebrew *qava,* can also be translated as 'hope'. In fact, the NIV Bible does translate this word as hope:

> *"but those who **hope** in the Lord will renew their strength. They will soar on wings like eagles; they will run and not grow weary, they will walk and not be faint."*
> Isaiah 40:31

It can also be translated as expect or to look for. This verse is not implying that those who simply 'wait' shall receive such strength and endurance. It implies that there is a direction, an object of the waiting. It is when our hope is centred on God himself that we may receive such sustenance. Which therefore means that maybe for those of us who have experienced that deflation, that 'sickness' on account of waiting, may not have had our hopes so squarely on God.

When I wrote my first book "Ministry Stinks" it was a time of great learning. I had ventured into very unknown territory. In fact, I didn't even know anyone who had written a book. And so every experience was new. I didn't know what to expect throughout the process, but I also didn't know which existing expectations I had adopted were unrealistic. And so I thought the book would sell, as they would say "like hotcakes". But of course, it didn't. Something strange happened at that time. I began following all these different Christian leaders, sending them books, hoping that one of them would read the book and therefore endorse it. I didn't realise how much their endorsement had gradually become 'my hope'. I began assessing my own worth and validity against whether they were liking my comments or replying to my attempts to contact.

Inevitably, I became very emotionally erratic. Because they weren't consistent in their responses. And furthermore, not one of them ever replied, thanked, responded, acknowledged or endorsed my book. In fact, one leader sent a letter back that condemned it in such a swift motion that it was impossible for them to have even read it. So they clearly either judged the book by its cover (which is no doubt a cheeky one) or they judged me.

As frustrating and disappointing as it all was, I had to confront that the placement of my hope had not actually been in God. It had been in them.

When God is our hope, we won't look for the signs or the typical milestones to validate us. We won't need to. Because we walk by faith and not by sight (2 Corinthians 5:7). When God is our hope, we can be patient because we know in His sovereignty that His plan is perfect and therefore His timing is perfect. When God is our hope, our own personal success and satisfaction become secondary to His name being glorified. We have renewed strength because we have surrendered the process. We have laid it down because He laid down His life on the cross at Calvary.

Chapter 5

Freedom

Sometimes our brokenness surprises us. Before moving interstate, I found myself embroiled in a conflict that I did not handle well. We were equally at fault, but because I have had a fair bit of experience in dealing with conflict, I hold myself at a higher level of responsibility. Sadly, I have had to confront that it may just be the end of that relationship. A soul-crushing possibility.

On the drive home, my husband tried to comfort me by giving me a 'balanced' view of the situation, concerned I'm sure that I heaped the responsibility far too much on my own side of the scale. But I knew better. The whole argument was because I said what I wanted to. Now how could that be a bad thing? Are we not meant to be authentic and real? Yes. But we aren't perfect in our perception of situations. We are judgemental, we are selfish and self-centred. We are broken and hurt, which was definitely the case for me at the time, unwisely failing to deal with the heavy emotions I was carrying from circumstances I never envisioned myself having to face.

When I say what I want to, it's being filtered through a whole lot of self-focused beliefs that have no concern for the other. And at that moment saying what I wanted was a completely self-motivated act. I really didn't care about the other person's feelings. I only cared about my own. And yet I thought it would turn out well? The truth is I wasn't even thinking about how it would turn out. And this was equally true for my 'adversary'.

Our knee jerk reactions are not necessarily wise. In fact, they rarely are. And so often they show us the faulty beliefs and dysfunctional feelings we have that lay beyond the surface. Often they show us that we are still very much on our own journey toward freedom.

How does freedom build a resilient faith?

One of the key issues presented by Jesus in the gospels is that the Pharisees and Sadducees had turned the law into a rigorous rule-oriented framework that was devoid of a genuine relationship with God. When Jesus arrived, so much of His priority was to clear the noise that these frameworks had created and to give clarity to what God really cared about. Jesus was so aware of how this previous tradition had weighed down the people, and He was interested in releasing them from the burden. His words are recorded in Matthew 11:28-30

> *"Come to me, all who labour and are heavy laden, and I will give you rest. Take my yoke upon you, and learn from me, for I am gentle and lowly in heart, and you will find rest for your souls. For my yoke is easy, and my burden is light."*

This passage spoke of the yoke that is laid upon oxen. In those days, a method of settling an unruly young ox was to place an implement over its body that attached it to an older ox. After kicking and fighting the young ox would eventually adjust to the calm and consistent walk of the older ox.

FREEDOM

It is unusual and yet somehow beautiful imagery of how we walk with Jesus, being tamed by His gentle kindness. Those who heard Jesus say this would have understood that the Greek word used here *phortizo* heavy laden, spoke of the fatigue you experience from an overburden with ceremony, rites and unnecessary precepts. It was the spiritual anxiety produced by the rigorous framework established by the religious leaders of that day. None of which actually brought the people closer to God. In fact, it was most likely to have placed a greater barrier between them and God, as it simultaneously caused them to misunderstand His nature. Jesus came and established these alternate refreshing ideas about God referring to Him as Father, describing himself as the Good Shepherd, as the Bread of Life. These ideas enhanced a relational framework for understanding God and brought His very nature to the forefront rather than clouded behind an onerous ceremonial system. As Paul states in Galatians 5:1

> *"For freedom Christ has set us free; stand firm therefore, and do not submit again to a yoke of slavery."*

Freedom was a significant part of Jesus' purpose in coming to earth. Not only because of the freedom from sin but the freedom from meaningless religiosity, which we might even call 'works'.

Paul again paints such a picture in Colossians 2:20-23

> *"If with Christ you died to the elemental spirits of the world, why, as if you were still alive in the world, do you submit to regulations - "Do not handle, Do not taste, Do not touch" (referring to things that all perish as they are used) - according to human precepts and teachings? These have indeed an appearance of wisdom in promoting self-made religion and*

asceticism and severity to the body, but they are of no value in stopping the indulgence of the flesh."

There were some serious doctrinal issues at the church of Colossae that threatened to undermine Jesus' work at the cross. In this passage, Paul is trying to draw attention to the allure of religious activity, in that it can appear wise and sacred but it offers no real hope against sin or devoted service to Christ.

What kinds of religious activity that appear wise and sacred might exist now? We often disregard such criticisms of our own generation because we believe our faith to be genuine. But this pervasive belief that something is not good enough, including ourselves, attracts this inane habit to add religious rules. It is hard for us to reconcile that the gospel is good enough on its own and that Jesus only requires a heartfelt response to His invitation as we relationally walk out His plans for our life, which we are completely reliant on Him to achieve. The simplicity of such a truth causes us to remark "well it's not that simple, we also have to do 'x, y' and 'z'". Do this over several generations and you've got much more than just 'xyz'. You have the whole alphabet!

A classic example is the daily reading of scripture. I'll be the first to say that reading scripture is the wisest of habits to establish. And whilst there are passages that certainly allude to a regular practice of being in the Word, there is nothing that so explicitly expresses the idea that we must daily read the scriptures. Often the passage in Joshua 1:8 is referred to in this discussion:

> *"This Book of the Law shall not depart from your mouth, but you shall meditate on it day and night, so that you may be careful to do according to all that is written in it. For then you will make your way prosperous, and then you will have good success."*

There were many kings in the Old Testament that forfeited the call of God because they were haphazard in applying the law. His instruction to Joshua was critical for the task He was leading the Israelites on. This was not the time for another 40 years of wandering, the promised land was in their sights and God was going to get them there. This word meditate is diminished when we assume it means 'read'. To meditate is a deeper consideration of the Word. It is not necessarily achieved by simply reading a passage. It requires reflection, deliberation, prayer and diligence to understand.

In my early stages of faith, I remember meditating on this passage. I had realised that such intense guilt and shame inhabited my time with God. Because if I had missed a day reading the Bible, I would feel disobedient. Condemned. So intense was this feeling, that I often feared to return to the Word the next day if I missed a day. When I considered this passage, I realised that this was never the intention of scripture reading. In fact, many parts of the scriptures were not even developed at the time of the Early Church. Personal devotional reading may not have been possible as often the scriptures were hand-copied for the one community. They would read the scriptures together when they were together. And even though the Jewish men were trained in the Torah from a young age, girls and women were excluded from Torah education. And Gentiles were excluded from the section of the temple where the Torah was read. To study scripture was not universally available. So why would this activity have a 'law-like' status, if it was impossible to achieve prior to the 1500s?

Devotional reading is a somewhat modern phenomenon. It is more critical now though, with our lives becoming increasingly independent and veering away from the regularity of community afforded in those days. But we ought not to add a 'rule' that was technically not mandated to the degree that we are often taught. For some, reading the Word is clouded.

There are many that use this activity to determine their level of righteousness. There are some that due to church trauma struggle to read scripture without painful memories clouding the activity. There are some that are riddled with guilt and condemnation at the activity, as was I.

God's purpose for us reading scripture is first and foremost, relationship. To know Him. It is His revelation to us, of who He is. With that in mind, the activity itself should not invoke feelings of guilt, shame, pain-related trauma or deem us morally superior or inferior.

In the last 15 years, and ever since meditating upon these scriptures, I have never opened the word of God because I should or because I feel guilt or some obligation. I may have gone a few days without reading it, but more often than not I am daily in the word, and sometimes several times a day (and not because I am a writer). When I am not reading it, I am often ruminating over verses and passages. It is rarely far from my mind. And it's not because I developed a habit of reading the Word. It's because I love God. I worked on love, and not simply the habit. Sometimes I open the Word and I feel like I can breathe as though I had not all day. I weep at its goodness. But my love for the Word didn't happen because I put a regimented rule on myself that I must read the Bible every day. I don't feel guilt, shame, pain or righteousness for having had a devotional time. I am not trying to alleviate some inner turmoil or sense of not feeling good enough. I simply want to know God and hear his voice. That's freedom. I don't follow a rule, where the inevitable risk is that the rule becomes our God. That's the risk with rules. Now the truth is we as Christians have hundreds if not thousands of these religious rules. Some are out of a personal conviction, and others have been passed down by tradition and culture. Point is, not all of them are so explicitly driven by God. Often, we haven't even wondered why we do it or if indeed it must be done. We follow the crowd, sometimes to protect our image, but we fail to realise that it is a religious rule that only makes us feel more restricted and does little to nullify the influence of sin in our life or to enhance a loving relationship with God. And before we know, it's the rule that is our Lord…not God.

That is why we must talk about freedom. At any given point, we are unaware of the rules we have accumulated that have nothing to do with God. And we have no hope at resilience when we are:

a) not free to pursue God without religious noise;
b) we are accommodating a whole bunch of activities that contribute nothing to our faith.

We ought not to assume that we are the freest versions of ourselves, right at this moment.

To begin with, we must talk about the greatest controller and limitation of freedom: SIN

Sin

Sin has been talked about extensively throughout the Christian community. It is as critical to the redemption story, as redemption itself. Many Christians have heard more about sin than they have the love of God. So, my intention in this section isn't to harp on about a very well-known concept. Or believe that I could theologically present something new. My intention is only this: to recognise that sin by far poses the biggest threat to freedom.

In my pre-Christian days, I believed that sin was my friend and that it offered me freedom. Instead, it offered me oppression and compulsion. Two conditions that are typified by a lack of control. When someone in authority comes along that controls a vulnerable individual, righteous anger rises within us as we fight for justice for that person. No better story could be told than that of Britney Spears, the world-renowned singer and artist. Britney was under a conservatorship governed by her father. She wasn't allowed to go anywhere or do anything or pay for anything without his authority. It began because of a mental health issue, but the authority continued well beyond necessity. In protest, social media, documentaries blitzed and chanted for Britney's freedom. Why did the world have such a response? Because we empathise with a full-grown human being controlled by a ruthless authority figure. It hurts us to have our free will taken away, especially when it is unwarranted. This is the equivalent of sin. It's the controller that we never asked for. But unfortunately, we inherit. Paul wasn't understating it when he used slave imagery to discuss the condition of sin.

It is a harsh ruler, an abuser that deceives us into believing it is our advocate. For the alcoholic, sin deceives them into believing that the drink will offer hope for relief. But it simultaneously tightens its hold on the drinker, becoming a physiological dependence. For the lustful, sin invites them into a world of pleasure misleading the lustful into thinking that pleasure could last forever or adequately fill the soul. But it only takes them deeper into the habit, demanding that they seek more and more experiences to feel good. Sin gaslights us. It manipulates us. It can own us.

Sin is the biggest threat to our freedom. Thanks be to God that we have grace given to us through Jesus' death on the cross. This is the only legitimate offer we have for freedom from sin. There was nothing in our own strength that we could do to remedy our situation. It's the grace and mercy of the Lord that makes a life of sinlessness possible.

When Adam and Eve were in the garden of Eden, they were without sin. The human body, soul and spirit was never designed with sin in mind. Sin is an offence to us. It's incompatible. Like new wine in an old wineskin.

FREEDOM

Therefore sin, in the long run, has a devastating effect on man and society. It is contrary to our design.

A few years ago, we had this gorgeous dog named Carl. Unfortunately, he only lived for 2 years because of a very severe case of epilepsy. Carl was an unusual dog. He would nip at us when we tried to discipline him. And he was abnormally fixated on his tennis ball. I had owned many dogs by this time, and I had never quite come across a dog like him. It was incredibly frustrating. Until we got a DNA test. We had been told he was a purebred Border Collie, even though he seemed like he had some German Shepherd in him. Apparently, he was an entirely different breed. One that I had never heard of. He was a Hungarian Vizsla, with just a little Border Collie in him. Of course, knowing his breed meant we could do a little research. We discovered that Carl probably didn't like me getting angry at him, as I sometimes would do. And Carl really liked to swim and be around other animals. We ended up taking him to a friend's farm, and Carl was in his element. I had never seen him like that! For starters he ran 10km and swam for 6kms when our friend decided to do some exercise. And secondly, he had this adorable fondness for the animals. Unlike our other border collie who would chase and bark at the animals, Carl would sit alongside the cows and the horses, following them as though he was one of them. We have this great photo of Carl gazing into the eyes of a stunning black horse and following him around a paddock. He also became much more obedient as I disciplined him differently. And he became so much more affectionate, often laying on my lap and gazing into my eyes.

I now say that he was the best dog I ever had! All in all, it was such a relief to have some understanding about his breed and release him to be the dog he was designed to be.

We understand this in dogs, but the breed of a dog significantly influences behaviours. Because many dogs were bred with a purpose, they don't seem quite right unless they are doing what they were bred to do. It's the same with us. There are certain things that sin brings into our lives that we were never purposed to deal with. We weren't meant to experience rejection. We weren't meant to experience loneliness. These are all emotions that didn't exist prior to sin. Again, sin is contrary to our design. That's why sin is the greatest barrier to freedom. When we sin, we are doing something that is harmful to us because it was never meant to happen. Even selfishness eventually erodes our inner being, because we are at our best when we love as designed by God.

Unfortunately, the world's impression of sin and the believer's prohibition of sinful acts is often seen as a restriction of freedom. Quite ironic, right? The world reasons that doing what you want is freedom. I would argue that this is a shallow interpretation of freedom and sin. With all the self-care discussions that ensue, we ought to consider that sin, if it is such an affront to our original design, is the opposite of self-care. Sin is a sign that you don't care about yourself. The interesting thing is that the desire to do and have whatever one feels is the very proof that sin controls us. It is proof that we are led by the flesh. And to be led by the flesh is to be enslaved to it and its compulsions. And what compels us, controls us. 2 Peter 2:19 says:

> *"They promise them freedom, but they themselves are slaves of corruption. For whatever overcomes a person, to that he is enslaved."*

The flesh doesn't care whether what you do is good for you, nor what consequences arise from following it. Genuine freedom is to be controlled by nothing. God himself doesn't seek to control us, He seeks to lead and for us to follow. God seeks to have us choose him, willingly. As our Lord. A Lord that is gentle and humble and serves. A Lord that won't manipulate us into staying, even if there is a threat that we will walk away. A Lord that willingly died on the cross for us, simply so we could be free of the shackle of sin that oppresses and torments us. This is the difference between submitted and controlled. Even though submission as a word has negative connotations these days, it still implies that the submitter is volunteering, giving permission, consenting to be led (submission gets a bad name, when it has been demanded). To be controlled is the opposite of voluntary. It is forced, coerced and manipulated.

Sin is the biggest threat to our freedom.

Fear

The country of Egypt has always fascinated me. In particular, ancient history involving pyramids, mummification, hieroglyphics…I have watched countless documentaries and read many articles. Although I want to visit Egypt someday, it would be somewhat pointless because of an irrational fear. I haven't spent the time trying to deal with and address this fear, because it hasn't proven to be so debilitating in my normal everyday life. But I'm sure it would be triggered in Egypt. I struggle with being in tight confined spaces. And to get into a pyramid, it often is primarily a tight confined space. So, the desire to go to Egypt has always been dampened somewhat for me by this one issue.

Fear, besides the fact that it is terribly uncomfortable, poses a threat to our freedom. For the most part we already know this. We know the lengths we go to, and the situations we avoid to feel safe and unafraid. But it is worth saying that for the person desiring to pursue freedom, which in essence should be all believers, fear would need to be addressed.

Again, we must acknowledge here that there is nothing in the garden of Eden or our original design that suggests that fear was a pre-sin phenomenon. In fact, there is more suggestion that fear occurs because of an occurrence that also was never designed for the human being: death. Our bodies have been designed with inbuilt systems to maximise our survival. We are constantly assessing threats to our livelihood. At its most basic level, fear is an emotion often with physical manifestations that is intended to protect us from perceived threats.

The body has inbuilt mechanisms for survival because we were never meant to die. Whether that be a spiritual death, a physical death, or even an emotional/psychological death. The scriptures tell us:

> *"He has planted eternity in the human heart..."*
> *Ecclesiastes 3:11 NLT*

In all of us, there is an innate desire to live. For eternity. Because we are made in the image of God, we are designed to be eternal beings, just as He is.

Recently we bought a kayak and had big plans to go out every weekend basking in the beautiful salty air of the ocean. Until a man sitting by the water told me that the body of water closest to us, was infested with bull sharks. I told my husband and he started doing some Google research to let me know that a shark attack had not been reported in more than 60 years. But it was enough to have me concerned. It's been some months with this back and forth of debate, with an elderly Aunty weighing in on her terrible experience seeing a shark in that exact body of water. Eventually my husband remarked to me that "Mel, if you are going to die by being eaten by a shark then it was always your way to go".

Now that may be true. Maybe it is a question of destiny. But regardless of how much I want to see Jesus, I still can't bring myself to swim with sharks. My whole-body recoils at the possibility. Because my whole being physically, mentally, emotionally or as the scriptures might describe it: mind, body and soul…desires to live. My fears are a survival mechanism to keep me safe. Now here's the problem: fear may be a function of survival, but what happens when our emotional and physical responses are all off? What happens when they are confused? What happens when trauma or circumstances have caused our fear response to be dysfunctional? Or even our fears are extreme and out of proportion? That is for the most part, a lot of what happens with an unhealthy fear. Seeing a car flying toward you at 100km/hour and the subsequent fear response we have, is probably healthy and a natural physical response. But thinking that all cars driving at 100km/hour will eventually crash into you, is an unreasonable fear.

Several years ago, I ended up developing an eating phobia. Yes, that's right, for 10 weeks I could not eat anything more than soups and drinks. I had seen several people choking over a short period of time, and it triggered something in me that I just couldn't control. It was a debilitating fear, and I experienced constant anxiety. So, I know a thing or two about unreasonable fears. And I know that I felt the threat of death every day, every time I ate. Even though I doubt the Apostle Paul was enduring such an unusual fear, I understood what it meant when he said:

> *"We were under great pressure, far beyond our ability to endure, so that we despaired of life itself. Indeed, we felt we had received the sentence of death."*
> 2 Corinthians 1:8-9 NIV

When we received Christ we started the new eternal life. Jesus states:

> *"I am the true bread that came down from heaven. Anyone who eats this bread will not die as your ancestors did (even though they ate the manna) but will live forever."* John 6:58 NLT

Yes, we experience physical death, but it is more like a transition than an annihilation. This is the miracle that Jesus has purchased for us through the cross at Calvary. In essence, nothing can actually kill us. Which is why so many that have been martyred before us, may have understood something that we don't always grasp: no one has the final say on your life. Not governments, not men and women intent on evil, not even sharks! Emperor Nero thought he could simply wipe out Christians and eradicate this new emerging group of believers. But he never really had the final say. He never really wiped any of them out, because you can't kill someone that cannot 'die'.

So, to be genuinely free from fear, we must fully embrace this gospel and this consequential truth: we are already resurrected. That which we fear, cannot really kill us. And if the worst-case scenario (death) is an impossibility, what power does that fear really hold over us?

Guilt and Shame

Just like our fear response, our experience of guilt can also become dysfunctional. There is relevance to guilt, in that it indicates to us a conflict of conscience. It is meant to cause us to repent. Unfortunately, the conscience can become overactive and even underactive, misconstruing events that either ought to cause guilt or ought not to cause guilt.

In my observations, this appears to affect Christians more than most. Because we often have more rules we consequently can have an overactive conscience. Feeling responsible for things that we aren't responsible for and feeling bad about things that we shouldn't.

And we ought not to underestimate the weight of unresolved or persistent guilt. It is a heavy burden to carry. We often don't recognise how many of our actions and choices are motivated by guilt. And many times, we risk disobeying God to alleviate guilt.

There is no greater example of the power of guilt, than that of Judas who after recognising the weight of his betrayal hung himself. Whilst Judas had done an incredibly evil act in handing Jesus over to the authorities, we know that this led to the cross, the very purpose of Jesus' earthly life. Maybe Judas may have been able to bounce back from this gross error in judgement. Maybe. Instead, his guilt was just far too heavy, and he consequently heaped his own version of punishment upon himself for his crime. Guilt is such a powerful emotion that it can cause us to sin further: a parent abandoning their family, escapism through the sins of lust and a host of other types of punishment we heap upon ourselves to serve as a recompense for our guilt. This can also be an attempt to assert some kind of pleasure as a temporary relief from guilt. Oftentimes, even a lack of attendance from church can be motivated by feelings of guilt.

Shame is equally as significant as guilt. In some ways, it may be even more potent in its ability to control our behaviours. Even though shame has been a discussion point in the world for a fair few years, Christians still seem to be relatively naive about the power of this emotion. Shame is the persistent belief of inadequacy and unworthiness. It's not necessarily motivated by the actions you do or do not take. If anything, actions or lack thereof, are used to affirm this existing internal declaration; you're not good enough. The feeling itself may often make a person want to hide, whether it be by creating distance between themselves and those things or people that make them feel vulnerable or even just being dishonest about who they are and things they do and think. It can cause embarrassment, intimidation, the desire to unreasonably please people and so much more. For so many believers, they don't realise that their pursuit to be good is often motivated by this feeling. Their desire to be righteous is to dull an internal sense of condemnation and unworthiness, and not just sheer worship to Jesus.

The fact is that both an overactive guilty conscience and shame are not experiences that have been endorsed by God.

> *"Therefore, there is now no condemnation for those who are in Christ Jesus."*
> Romans 8:1 NIV

Our status in Christ is FORGIVEN. We are no longer condemned, even when we sin. To be condemned is to be worthy of punishment, it is to have a sentence issued for a crime. But on account of Jesus' sacrifice none of us in Christ, are now liable to pay the debt of our sin or be issued a sentence for it. An overactive guilty conscience not only places us as responsible for a non-existent crime, but it also can mean holding ourselves in a place of punishment that Jesus does not authorise. And shame is like having placed yourself permanently in a jail cell when no conviction exists.

These two are very powerful emotions that frequently contort our impressions of freedom, and our ability to experience it.

We cannot ignore the influence that our emotions have on our experience of freedom. Because freedom, according to the New Testament, is a status. We are declared free, it is a position we hold. It is not determined by whether we feel good or feel bad. It doesn't change because we have become more or less 'righteous'. It is not determined by our reasoning, our calculations of where we stand according to how we feel. It is granted by God. I have never been the kind to advocate ignoring our emotions, that has caused more harm than we are willing to admit. But I do believe that this is what it means to consider ourselves in light of God's pronouncements.

And God's pronouncements are true and accurate, because He doesn't lie. In fact, He can't lie since it is contrary to His nature.

Learning to Rely on God

The Apostle Paul says this very odd thing in response to his own struggles with what many believe was possibly depression or even a mental breakdown. As we continue in the second part of 2 Corinthians 1:9 he says:

> *Indeed, we felt we had received the sentence of death.* ***But this happened that we might not rely on ourselves but on God****, who raises the dead.*

The Apostle Paul reasons that the goal is to rely on God, and not on ourselves. But what does it mean to really truly rely on God? While in ministry, people would talk about relying on God as though He was the source of some energy injection when you were fatigued from serving. But beyond that there weren't a lot of specifics. Maybe it doesn't need explanation, maybe it's more straight forward than I think. But either way I have taken the time to examine what exactly it means to rely on God:

- Trusting Him for His timing instead of rushing ahead in zeal or impatience.
- Trusting Him to open and close doors to opportunities, instead of trying to force opportunities to happen by your own efforts.
- Trusting Him for healing and allowing Him to guide you toward your breakthrough.
- Trusting Him to sanctify you, grow you and form you as you simply put yourself in a position to be changed.

- Trusting Him to provide financially and refrain from overwork and deceptive acts.
- Trusting Him with your children and not attempting to push or manipulate them into living for Christ.
- Trusting Him for your future, knowing that He will always be your Good Shepherd.
- Trusting God with your marriage that He who began a good work in your spouse will carry it onto completion, and therefore not chastising or criticising your spouse's relationship with God.
- Trusting Him for your ministry, that He will provide and speak through you, connect you with the right people.

You may have your own specific examples based on your context of what it means to rely on God. None of this is possible without the Holy Spirit and relying on God doesn't mean that you do NOTHING. We faithfully do what God has asked us to do in this moment, even if that direction is to rest. Relying on God simply means recognising that which only God can do and allowing Him the space to do that which only He can do.

To close this chapter, let me remind you that we ought to pursue real freedom. The freedom that doesn't look to add rules where there is no need to. The freedom that seeks not to sin. The freedom that is fearless. The freedom that is without guilt and shame. And to rely on God during our battles to gain that freedom. Freedom not only changes your perspectives about life, it also produces a resilience that is able to handle life. None of us thrive in our faith the more inwardly contained we are. We thrive when we can freely worship in Spirit and in Truth.

Chapter 6

Community

"Tashi And the Monk" was a documentary released in 2014 following the story of the former Buddhist Monk Lobsang Phunstok.[8] He founded a school home 'Jhamtse Gatsal' atop a mountain in the Himalayas. In Tibetan this means 'The Garden of Love & Compassion'. With 85 students the school often took in children who had lived in extreme poverty, sold or neglected by their parents. The children often begin their time at Jhamtse Gatsal with behavioural issues, acting out due to the inner turmoil they have experienced for having been unwanted. But as they are immersed in this loving and caring environment where their 'siblings' also support and encourage them, given grace and gentle correction…these behaviours dissipate and they are free to focus on study and the hopes of a brighter future. It is a powerful story that demonstrates the significance that community plays in both healing and direction. This example demonstrates how the environment alone can be a single

---

[8] Tashi & The Monk (2014)

factor as to whether someone lives a successful life, or one where poverty becomes a cyclical process.

As Christians in the Western world, we understand that community is important, but we underestimate its significance. We wouldn't assume that community would be an integral part of a person's recovery. We wouldn't assume that having a community would provide us with identity and a sense of security. We wouldn't assume that having a community would provide us with the kind of love that would cease that inner warring and striving that is often motivated by a desire to be seen and known.

I have often looked at the New Testament in awe at how followers of Jesus in that day were willing to give up their very life for the gospel, wondering what was in them, what conviction did they have or understanding had they gained in order to live like this? But it is only recently that I have realised that the community where they felt support and encouragement to love and serve God was a significant factor in their ability to face the persecution that surrounded them.

Churches have underestimated the significance of community, a fact that I often would lament over when I was the Small Groups Pastor in a medium to large sized church. The focus was so frequently on the service, the order, the preaching, the worship, stage transitions…the part of the week where most church members were 'passive'. Not realising that in most cases the greatest selling point for a church to a new person is the experience of the community, regardless how great the preaching was and regardless how great the worship is. I once had a friend say to me that they didn't need to go to church anymore to hear 'good' preaching, or great worship with all the formats out there to obtain good preaching and worship.

The only thing that could not be experienced, that was irreplaceable was the community. And yet the influence of a community is still underplayed.

COMMUNITY

New Christians are reliant on community. The Apostle Paul uses the imagery of a baby to describe the reliance that a new Christian has on the Body of Christ and the Holy Spirit. They literally cannot survive the first stages of their faith, independently. And yet it can be a struggle to find people to journey alongside a new Christian.

See, the fact is that God always intended for this new covenant to create an inherent design for community. The Spirit joins us to each other, and to God. It is virtually an unbreakable connection (besides renunciation). It is not dependent on our awareness of this connection or whether we choose to gather with those within that connection. What makes the difference is the degree to which we are aware of this innate connection and the degree to which we identify with the communities we find ourselves in. I have had the privilege of walking with a significant number of Millennials and Gen Zed's over the last 3-5 years who unfortunately have walked away from Christian community despite their Christian upbringing. They still believe in Jesus. They still have Christian friends. They still read the word. But they refuse to return to a church. When I talk to them about this, I can see that offence is rarely the cause, as preachers tend to suggest. And even when I use my counselling skills to sift through the behaviours, body language and comments, I can't see any evidence of offence. They often do demonstrate signs of disillusionment, something I have covered extensively in my second book. But eventually they arrive at this place where they comment on their inability to see themselves in a modern church. Which in essence means that they are unable to identify with the values of the modern church. For many it's the perceived hypocrisy of attesting to love thy neighbour, but lack of compassion for the LGBQTIA community and even hatred in some respects. For others it's the aggressive 'empire-building' that they perceive of modern churches. And for others it's the continual missional messages, but the inability to provide a genuinely safe judgement-free environment for their non-believing friends to visit. Whatever the reason, their perception of what the modern church represents is not something they believe they can identify with.

There are also those within the church who rarely feel like they fit in. They don't feel as though they identify with the cliques. I have often seen this happening with the youth in a church community more than any other group. There are the 'good' Christian kids, and everybody else. And if you aren't one of the 'good' ones, you are more likely to identify as 'bad' and therefore hang out with the kids that feel misunderstood, rejected and overlooked. All of which is detrimental to the psyche of those kids. Because none of them are bad! And as far as God is concerned, they aren't any worse than the 'good' Christian kids. And they may not have even been rejected, but they exclude themselves because they don't identify with what is praised and rewarded. But worst of all, it gives them an inaccurate impression of how God relates to all of us. He doesn't compare us like this. He doesn't need us to become someone to be loved by Him. He doesn't reject us based on our behaviour. But unfortunately, those labels and assumptions stay with these kids right into adulthood, forming and framing their experiences and beliefs.

Community is far more critical in the successful walk of a believer than most factors we presume to be critical. It is therefore also essential that we explore this concept of community in relationship with resilience.

How does community enhance our resilience in faith?

A friend of mine was recently telling me about her community. A group of couples that regularly get together to eat, to celebrate, to laugh and enjoy each other's company. They support each other with babysitting, meals when one is unwell, and friendship. The primary uniting factor? Ethnicity. We both grew up as the main non-white children in our class and understand what it is like to come from very strong cultures with a rich history and adapt to a western culture that often expects assimilation. I am probably not fully aware of the degree to which I have lost my own original identity in order to survive in the western culture that I have grown up in, partly because I was also born into this culture. But for her, she migrated after birth, she notes that she felt the pressure even to fabricate her accent. So, I am really thankful that she has found the community she has. It is the only environment where she doesn't have to pretend to be someone else to survive emotionally. She can relax in her community, be herself, without having to contort herself to be understood.

Can you imagine if she had to 'perform' or pretend, when it came to her faith community? She has had to do this, as have I. But what kind of messages could she interpret from such a scenario? That she needs to 'perform' for God? That she must assimilate to be accepted? That she must keep some areas of her life hidden from God?

The biggest reason we need community on our journey with resilience, is that when resilience is our goal we actually can't pretend anymore. Because faking faith doesn't produce resilience. In fact, faking it prevents resilience. When we fake it, we deny those predetermined parts of ourselves to be amenable to a crowd. That's not resilience! When times of hardship come, those things that were denied can upend us.

Now I have used such a complicated topic to exemplify the difficulties with belonging. Multiculturalism is such a complex factor to negotiate within a western church. Because often the experience of a culturally based minority group is not influenced by the church experience alone. It is part of a broader experience of the country where they are the minority.

I say this to acknowledge the complexities that such an example gives rise to, but not necessarily to provide any answer to that in this small space.

The point is, that we need community in our resilient faith journey because we need to stop pretending for our own sakes. And the right kind of community can help us stop pretending.

PLEASE NOTE...

Before I proceed, I must state this very critical fact: not all communities are healthy for us. We know this intuitively when we consider gangs, the mafia, white-supremacist groups, the KKK or even just those groups on Tik Tok that encourage extreme dieting to 13-year-olds! Additionally, not all Christian communities are healthy for us too. Sometimes churches get distracted and they forget why they exist; to equip the Body of Christ to do good works. And so I want to offer you some points to help you in determining whether you should stay in a given community:

- **God has given you some kind of indication that you should be here.**

    In my last two churches, I have had multiple dreams that have clearly indicated to me that this is the church we were to attend. Therefore prayer cannot be discounted in the process of finding the right community. I have still gone through some difficult experiences, but at least I have known that God has meant for me to attend even if it was for a season. Now I realise that not every person hears God like this, but prayer is still a very relevant part of the process.

- **How are congregation members motivated?**

    Most churches are trying to motivate you to live for God. Whether it be by becoming more missional, whether it is to read the Word more, whether it is to pray more, to give more, to volunteer, to serve. It's not necessarily a manipulative thing, but for some churches it can become so. The best reason to do any of these expressions of faith is as an overflow from the wholesome loving relationship that you have with God. You desire to worship Him, and therefore you serve, give, pray, read the Word etc.

But unfortunately, just as the world can do, some churches will use fear to motivate you. Whether it's the fear of chastisement, or the fear of exclusion and judgement. Some churches may use guilt to motivate, suggesting that you aren't a good enough Christian unless you do the things, they are proposing that you do. Others might motivate using duty, that you ought to do this if you call yourself a Christian. To be fair, Paul wrote things that reminded us of our duty as believers so all in all, duty is not the worst thing. But I have never seen guilt or fear lead to a healthy theology of God and how He intends for us to relate to Him.

So, either the leaders of a church have been so driven to meet their goal that they are using ungodly tools to get there, or they themselves struggle with fear and guilt that they unknowingly project onto others. The latter we can have grace for, but it's very hard not to get caught up in that web of fear and guilt if it is very pervasive. All of us still struggle with fear and guilt to some degree, so we can't expect a church to be completely fearless and guilt-free in their messaging. Although we would hope it is always getting better. Steer clear of the extremes of fear and guilt as motivators for action. In the long run that is not going to be a healthy environment.

- **How gracious are they?**

    It is hard to consider this sometimes, when you look around at the state of the church at large, but grace is meant to be a hallmark of the Christian community. Not only that supernatural grace that God gives us on account of Jesus, but the grace we are to extend to one another. In the New Testament we are encouraged to be patient with one another (Ephesians 4:2; Colossians 3:13), to bear one another's burdens (Galatians 6:2) and forgive one another (Ephesians 4:2; Ephesians 4:32). We are told not to judge one another (Romans 14:13), do not slander one another (James 4:11) and not to grumble against each other (James 5:9). Are these not all expressions of grace and graciousness?

    You can pick up on the graciousness of a community very easily. It's in the things they say. Do they talk about other people in the 'world' with judgement? How do they handle when someone falls short of their standard or plan? Is there pride? Do they go on about the people they know and the connections they have? Do they keep a record of their successes before the congregation?

- **How mentally healthy are the staff?**

    I once had a parent tell me to check out the health and attitude of the staff in a day care centre, before I decide to leave my kids there. I couldn't quite understand how that would flow on to affect the kids, but since having my daughter in two different day care centres I can see it makes a massive difference. The principle is the same with churches. Christians often make the mistake of looking at the Senior Pastor to determine whether it's a good community to join. But the people underneath him or her, are far better indicators of the health of a church and what the church truly stands for. For starters, how tired are the staff? They will be tired, whether it's a big church or a small church. But how tired are they? And is it persistent? Do they take breaks? Do they take holidays?

What do they expect of themselves to be able to achieve? Are they free to say 'no'? Or is it so culturally ingrained that you must say yes, that nobody would even think to say 'no'? I'm essentially talking about boundaries here. Can the staff member make boundaries and that boundary be respected? Is workaholism encouraged? Is the environment so driven that it could blur the lines of appropriateness? Is there a rigid hierarchy? Are the staff extreme people pleasers?

You aren't going to find a perfect church. And in fact, none of us should have the goal of finding a perfect church since even God himself is not looking for a perfect Bride, but only a Bride that is ready. And some of the above pointers I have listed aren't going to be recognisable to you on the first few visits. Or you may never know the answer to some of these questions. But in fact, the internal subconscious radar is still going to blink: 'do I identify with what is presented here?'

However, there is one question that is not typically asked when considering the types of communities worth joining.

Iron Sharpens Iron

Proverbs 27:17 states this compelling principle:

> *Iron sharpens iron, and one man sharpens another.*

This passage is often spoken at weddings, but besides then it is not often a verse that is referred to. It's no Jeremiah 29:11, or John 3:16! And yet it describes with such poignant imagery, the effect friendship can have. Iron and iron, means they are two equals. And in the process of friction or contact, they improve and refine each other. There are two issues that are necessary to discuss before we proceed with such an idea. On the one hand, society tells us that a good friendship makes you feel good. But on the other hand, often in Christian community we can presume that refining each other means harsh chastisement. Both are extreme interpretations of friendship. Iron does indeed sharpen iron, but it doesn't happen by polishing the iron nor by smashing it. It is a healthy thing for friends to challenge each other, especially when it is done with kindness. I have been deliberate not to say 'love', because we as Christians have often used that statement as a scapegoat for rough treatment. Saying that we are doing something out of love that damages someone, is not love.

With that being said, I can now proceed with my thoughts that this verse is a helpful philosophy in approaching any spiritual community, and in particular Christian friendships. It surprises me how often people will make friends and hang out with other Christians assuming that this will have a positive impact on their life…just because they are Christian. But not every Christian friendship has the 'iron sharpens iron' effect. Some Christian friendships are harmful to our faith. It may not necessarily be because of the other person, sometimes some friendships seem to bring out the worst in us. I am not typically a people pleaser, but for some reason there are maybe one or two friends that I have had in the past that I really seemed to need to please. Thankfully they never asked me to do anything I felt uncomfortable with, but I did find myself feeling as though I was at their mercy. But even more so, I just never want to believe that I need to please anyone besides God. That's a temptation I am not willing to expose myself to. So I don't spend much time with them these days. Sadly, I think many Christian people are so desperate to fit in and not feel so lonely that they compromise on what constitutes a good Christian friend. Worse still, many Christian people don't take the time to consider what it means to be a Christian friend as the Bible would describe it. This shows how we completely misunderstand the value of friendship. A whole book could be dedicated to this topic alone, but in this section, I will simply offer you three points:

1. **Friends are faithful to each other**

    The scriptures tell us in Proverbs 18:24

    One who has unreliable friends soon comes to ruin, but there is a friend who sticks closer than a brother. NIV

    A true friend won't forget that you exist or only come alongside you when you are doing well. They will stick closer than a sibling. They are there through tough times and even when the other is struggling to be faithful to God. Ecclesiastes 4:10 says *If either of them fall down, one can help the other up.* Christian friendships support each other even when one stumbles.

2. **Friends are trustworthy**

    Proverbs 16:28:

    A perverse person stirs up conflict, and a gossip separates close friends.

A true friend won't gossip about you but will also refuse to listen to gossip. I have a few friends like this, and I love them dearly. I trust them completely. Even when they have said something to me that I could have been offended by, I am able to look past my feelings because I trust their love for me. This kind of friendship is a gift that I return and hope to give to others.

But trustworthy doesn't only mean the keeping of confidences. It also means being trustworthy in our response to our friends' confidences. Job 6:14 reminds us that *a good friend does not withhold mercy and kindness*. Our friends should be able to trust or even predict that they will find kindness when they share their stories with us. Even their deepest darkest secrets. Because sharing contributes to our healing. James 5:16 tells us that we ought to:

Confess your sins to one another and pray for each other, that you may be healed. NIV

How we respond matters. Proverbs 16:24 *Gracious words are like a honeycomb, sweetness to the soul and health to the body.*

3. **Friends love and encourage**

Proverbs 17:17 says this incredible fact: *A friend loves at all times.* What a high value God places on friendship, with such a statement.

I have held this value of friendship in the highest of regards throughout my life. Church ministry does make it hard when you are so busy with so many people, but the truth is I have tried to be a good friend my entire life. I hold it as equal in value to my call as a minister. And the very substance of the call to love my neighbour. Take a moment to consider how valuable friendship truly is in this life. A good conversation with a friend could prevent a person from suicide. A good friendship can make another believe in themselves again. A good friend can help someone be faithful to their spouse. A good friendship could make someone believe in Jesus again. All the critical moments in life are often made lighter through friendship.

Similarly, we can find Christian communities where the act of 'iron sharpening iron' is a collective experience. The influence of a good community can change us. In fact, we have the ability to grow with each other. The truth is even non-Christian communities can influence people to grow and heal. Like we see in support groups: Alcoholics Anonymous, Gamblers Anonymous, Narcotics Anonymous, and so many more. But Christian communities all the more, when we are equally pursuing God with the power and presence of the Holy Spirit leading and guiding us all. This is the greatest reason to be a part of a healthy Christian community. The truth is the right community combined with a willing heart, can produce a faith in us much like what has been described frequently throughout this book. It can produce a faith that persists through every trial regardless of how severe and crippling the challenge. We hear of it every day. Of believers who endure the most distressing or sorrowful situations because they had a family of believers rallying around them with prayer, care and support.

This is the kind of community that we all at heart really crave for. The 'iron sharpens iron' community.

Modelling

This kind of community doesn't come easily. We also must contribute to it, to create it. By being the community, we want to receive. The hard truth is that this kind of community starts with us. We model the kind of community we want to see, the one that is represented in scriptures.

This is a biblical principle that we learn about in Sunday School:

> *So in everything, do to others what you would have them do to you, for this sums up the Law and the Prophets.*
> *Matthew 7:12 NIV*

As believers, we are encouraged to make the first move. We treat others as we would hope to be treated. We become the community that we want to experience. We become 'iron sharpens iron' friends, and we cultivate that kind of community amongst our own friends, our small group and church. There are many believers who will talk about the community that they want to experience, but there are much fewer who are willing to be that community for others. But that is what indicates that we are genuine followers of Jesus: we do first. Despite the reaction we get, we initiate. Just as Christ died, while WE were still sinners.

The reason Jesus asks us to initiate, to take the first step, is because love will make you do that. Because not only does He want us to be motivated by love, but He wants us to be models of good works in this life and not wait for something to happen to us before we do what is good and right.

As you can imagine my daughter is given a healthy dose of education from myself about friendship. I am happy that she tries her best at school, but I am way more interested in how she interacts with other kids. Recently she told me this story about how this little girl kept asking her to show her nails to her. My daughter has pretty nails, and they grow super-fast…so we aren't always on top of cutting her nails. But my daughter was complaining about how annoying it is. So let me relay this conversation, as it will be much easier than trying to explain:

Me: "Well maybe you could just avoid her when you see her coming"

Daughter: "She only says it when I go to her"

Me (in disbelief): "Why are you going to her if you don't like her asking about your nails?"

Daughter: "I go to her when she is by herself and hasn't got anyone to play with"

Me (after a few minutes of melting inside with pride and adoration for my daughter): "Wait, is that when you are by yourself and have no one to play with?"

Daughter: "No. Even if I am with my friends, if she's by herself I go and talk to her"

Me...further melting

END SCENE

I can't explain to you how proud I was of my little girl. She will never have to come home and prove to me that she is smart with grades, awards and accolades. I am satisfied with her being a great friend to her fellow human. And I will model that to her for the rest of my life.

The reason I value friendship so much is because I am a product of my friends. Every couple of years I write a teary text to my friends thanking them for the example of Christian friendship that they showed that little Hindu girl all those years ago. I was different. I was strange. I had completely different experiences and even homelife to them. But they included me, loved me, cared for me and carried me through some really tough times. I know that friendship is powerful, because it has saved me from all kinds of challenges. When I didn't think life was worth it, when I almost gave up on my faith. I didn't have a Christian family, and even sometimes I didn't have a church building and leaders to guide me through those times. My friends were my church.

Last Thoughts

Jesus said this remarkable thing whilst he was here on earth, he said:

> *Greater love has no one than this: to lay down one's life for one's friends. You are my friends if you do what I command. I no longer call you servants, because a servant does not know his master's business. Instead, I have called you friends, for everything that I learned from my Father I have made known to you.*
> *John 15:13-15*

Jesus held the concept of friendship in such high regard, that he used it to describe what He calls the greatest of loves. He goes on to say that He calls us friends. He sacrificed His life for His friends. Friendship is a sacred relationship that Jesus uses to describe how He sees us.

For the sake of my Christian friends who are journeying through their own disillusionment with the church, I have been clear to say that friendship is at the heart of community. Which may or may not come from a church, although I hope it does. But if you don't have a church to attend, please be sure to have a community of friends who will provide that 'iron sharpens iron' environment for you. If you don't have that, do everything you can to find it. Otherwise, it may be time to become 'iron sharpens iron' for others. The resilience of our faith relies on it.

Chapter 7

Managing Emotions

Have you ever had one of those pieces of clothing or accessory that seems to get caught on everything? I used to have this handbag that would get caught on door handles, door jams, hooks and any kind of protruding paraphernalia when you walked past it. I don't know if it was due to the way I was holding it, or whether it was the bag itself. But somehow, I would end up looking like a dope as I tried to walk forward only to be yanked unexpectedly back. If I simply pulled hard with force, I would damage the bag.

This is what emotions can be like when they are mishandled. You're really not going anywhere, until you unfasten yourself from the emotion that remains hooked. Simply pushing yourself without self-compassion can lead you to a disastrous place. Precision and care is required to safely resolve emotions that keep us stuck on the event that precluded it.

I am going to be quite bold here and say that there may not be anything that poses a greater threat to resilience in our faith than how we handle our emotions. And the risk is two-fold:

1. The risk of not understanding how to appropriately handle an unwanted emotion.
2. The risk of simply pretending the emotion isn't there and invalidating it.

Either we over-accentuate the influence of emotions by our lack of understanding, and therefore in the long run we make them more consequential than they need to be. Or we undervalue them by failing to acknowledge them. Often people in this latter category see emotions as a barrier to serving God or have been told that certain emotions are ungodly. The Christian populace tends to veer on this side of the scale more than the former.

Whichever category we tend to find ourselves leaning toward, the risk of further damage is there. It is critical to the journey of having a resilient faith that we learn how to appropriately manage our emotions.

Emotions and God

Christian people over many generations have found restoration in reading the Psalms. Whether David is lamenting, or he is rejoicing, the Psalms have given the permission to acknowledge emotions. And yet as a Christian society we still have so much difficulty in general, with expressing or acknowledging our emotions. We are fine with some emotions, but not all. We love joy. But we hide sadness. We love calmness. But we are repulsed by anger. We love amusement. But we hate confusion.

But in all our frustrations with emotions, we miss this truth: we have emotions because God also has emotions. Okay to be clear I'm not sure if God experiences all the emotions we do, I can't really be certain of that. But Jesus displays many emotions that we are often uncomfortable with in our own lives, despite Him being a perfect human being. He wept. He mourned. He got angry. He even appeared depressed in one case when He told His disciples that His soul was sorrowful to the point of death (Matthew 26:38).

So, in a general sense we cannot discount our emotions as though they are an interruption because Jesus had them and did not treat them as one. We have obviously been given them for a reason. So, what is the role and purpose of emotions?

Signs and Symptoms

How do you know if you have the flu? You know because there are a host of symptoms typically associated with the flu. Achy muscles, cold, cough, fever, headache…these are symptoms because our body reacts a certain way to having a problematic organism residing within it. This reaction, these symptoms are like a means of communication to us to know that something is amiss.

Emotions are like the symptoms of our heart. Our heart utilises emotions to communicate with us and indicate that something is occurring within it. It doesn't discern the rightness or wrongness of what is happening inside, it simply communicates it. Emotions give us some idea of how our heart is interpreting a situation, the world and our lives. So, when someone becomes angry, it might be an indication that the person has interpreted the situation as a threat or they are feeling unheard. When one becomes nervous or anxious, it may indicate that the person has interpreted the situation as vulnerable or precarious. This makes it quite strange that we in Christian culture habitually tend to ignore or even constrain our unwanted emotions. If we change our emotional perspective coming to see it as a warning system, a method of notifying us of deeper heart matters that may need to be considered, we might not be so hasty to dismiss its notifications. We would see that we rely on this system to walk out our faith.

> "Guard your heart above all else, for it is the source of life."
> Proverbs 4:23 CSB

Anything that gives us awareness of what is in our hearts, is a blessing. It gives us an opportunity to genuinely 'guard our heart'.

> "Keep your heart with all vigilance, for from it flow the springs of life." ESV

One might argue that paying attention to our emotions and responding to their signals, is exactly how we become vigilant over our hearts as this version suggests. Often as believers we will try to 'guard' the springs, managing the emotions, instead of guarding our hearts. We do this because:

a) Our culture has taught us that we ought to be uncomfortable with certain emotions and so managing that unwanted emotion becomes our focus.
b) We are often more preoccupied with hiding these emotions from our peers because of cultural distaste for these emotions.
c) Due to the overarching tendency of shallowness in our society, we simply try to move on quickly instead of taking the time to do the deep work of understanding and healing our hearts.

But our hearts have something to say. Proverbs 4:23 shows us that the heart is the source of all. And God values and cares deeply for our hearts, in fact it is:

- Where he writes his law (Jeremiah 31:33)

- Where love comes from (Matt 22:37)
- Where we believe (Mark 11:23)
- Where we treasure and ponder (Luke 2:19)
- Where rivers of living water flow from (John 7:38)

Our hearts are highly influential whether it is in a positive or negative way. On this basis, we cannot afford to ignore its signals to us. Because we are all essentially stewards of our hearts.

See it's not the emotions that are the problem, it's the actions that come out of the emotions that are of concern to God. Much to the amazement of many believers, God doesn't deny anger. Biblical characters are often expressing anger. And even in Ephesians 4:26 the Apostle Paul states:

"Be angry and do not sin; do not let the sun go down in your anger"

This verse makes it clear that we can be angry emotionally, but we aren't to act on that anger. Because anger, when it overpowers and progresses into action, could cause you to gossip, seek vengeance or hate. All acts that are considered sin. The second part of this verse implies that there is a correct way to manage an emotion like anger. It implies that anger is not something that is assisted by the passing of time. Anger requires active and early intervention. Even though the verse doesn't give us specific and practical advice on how to address anger before the sun goes down at the very least it demonstrates for us that anger as an emotion, is not inherently wrong. When we struggle to understand how anger could be a normal emotion, it is an indication of our own confused relationship with anger. Which would be likely in someone who has been exposed to domestic violence, or they have other issues with confrontation and intimidation.

Sometimes as believers, we can be like this with emotions in general. For a long time, unbeknownst to me, I took great efforts to tell people that I wasn't a typically emotional person. This was because I had seen high levels of uncontrolled emotion in my upbringing and didn't want to identify with it. I've seen this as well with other believers. Where they may have had a tense relationship with an emotional family member, and therefore deny their own emotions because they've learnt emotions are bad. Whilst that may serve us for a time, to help us survive the situations we are in particularly in childhood, in the long run it is not a helpful practice. It would be to our benefit to get rid of these labels that define a person's level of 'emotion' in a negative light, because it doesn't help in giving people permission to express emotions when they really need to.

The Risky Ones

Before I proceed in suggesting appropriate ways to deal with emotion, I think it would be pertinent to mention the emotions that are most likely to derail our journey of resilience. By doing so, I hope that I might be able to increase your awareness and increase prevention.

1. **Loneliness**

    The deception that people believe when they are lonely, is that they are the only one who feels alone. Loneliness is experienced by us all. And sometimes the more well-known you are, the more loneliness you experience. Loneliness isn't about how many friends you have. Some of the loneliest people have the most active social lives. And marriage doesn't fix loneliness either. You could be lying in bed next to the person of your dreams, and still feel like the loneliest person on earth. Okay, you might have less chance of feeling lonely, but company doesn't remove the possibility of loneliness.

Loneliness is a multilayered experience. We can experience loneliness because we don't feel understood, we don't feel seen, known, valid or heard. We can experience loneliness because we don't feel like anyone identifies with our story. Which is why often knowing other people in similar circumstances to you makes such a significant difference. And of course, it can be related to isolation and physical distance. But not all forms of loneliness have the same effect on your choices and actions. Severe loneliness can cause you to consider options that are terribly unhealthy for you. Like dating someone you know you shouldn't. Or staying in an unhealthy situation because it's better than being alone. Loneliness can make you want to give up mentally, and even physically. Loneliness is one of the most unpleasant and influential emotions that can be experienced.

If you experience loneliness, it's important to understand that loneliness is contributed to by a lack of intimacy. It's the quality of your relationships that count. Are you able to be vulnerable, honest and fully yourself? And when you are, do you feel validated, understood, heard, seen and known? That is intimacy. And that is usually what is lacking when you feel alone.

We know that God often intends for us to be by ourselves, like when the Apostle Paul spent three years in Arabia prior to going to Jerusalem to meet the Apostles (Galatians 1). King David spent a lot of time alone throughout his life. He was alone in the fields as a shepherd boy. He was alone when he travelled to the battlefield to bring food to his brothers. And then of course when he was being pursued by Saul, he was alone for some time hiding in caves.

So there is purpose in some loneliness, as a form of developing intimacy with Christ. Which makes sense, because if we are constantly surrounded by people and pursuing intimacy with others we don't get the chance to develop an intimate relationship with Christ. But it is still possible to experience loneliness even when you have Jesus. Because whilst God can fill our needs for intimacy, God also intends for us to experience relationships and intimacy with each other and through the Body of Christ.

But in general, loneliness can lead us toward an abandoning of faith in that it may cause us to take such drastic measures to fill the void that either tempts or exposes you to influences that detract from faith.

2. **Pain and Sorrow**

We all experience pain and sorrow at some point in life. Whether from the loss of a loved one, or a marital breakdown, or any other major event. But we even feel pain on a day-to-day basis, with everyday things: being left out of the party, not feeling good enough, or because of past trauma. Yes, they often do stem from other emotions, like shame and guilt, but experientially it just feels like pain or inner turmoil. For some people, this pain is persistent. They feel it often. For others it's situational. But again, extreme pain and sorrow are very influential feelings. It is hard to function when you have these feelings. People do crazy things when they are in pain, often with some deep desire to alleviate pain. They take drugs. They binge drink. They impulse buy. And of course they can take out their pain on others, bullying, physical abuse, emotional abuse and of course sexual abuse.

Pain or even the fatigue resulting from a lack of relief, can so easily derail your faith.

3. **Betrayal**

    There are very few things as painful and confusing as betrayal. It does something to us that cuts deep. When it's deliberate, it's absolutely shocking. To know that someone might intend to hurt us? What a horrendous thought. And when it's unintentional, it doesn't change the feeling besides maybe making us feel a bit ripped off because we aren't as justified in staying upset. Betrayal can make us do many unhealthy things. Betrayal can fixate us on the situation, with great struggles to move forward. It can make us bitter, or resentful. It can make us seek revenge, punishment or just a desire to balance the scales, taking joy in the misfortune of our betrayer. And of course it can make you give up on our faith, especially if you have been naive enough to assume that betrayal may never happen to you. The expectation that following God might make you avoid hardships in life, can make something like betrayal even more devastating causing what you believed about God and what it means to be a Christian, to come under scrutiny.

4. **Rejection**

    Could anything make us feel smaller than rejection? It doesn't matter if the rejection is because of an unfashionable hairstyle, or because someone doesn't like your personality…rejection makes us feel weak, insignificant and worthless. It is one of the hardest experiences to bounce back from, because it drills deep into our confidence and emotional security. The crazy fact about rejection is that even a small amount of rejection can cause us to walk away from God. We just don't always realise that it was a previous rejection that did it. The desire to keep up with the Joneses, the desire to be considered cool or pretty, the desire to be seen as intellectual can all stem from some previous rejection. And in each case, if the desire to demonstrate one's sufficiency is persistent enough one could compromise their faith. It is entirely possible to be so taken with keeping up with the Joneses that our faith becomes secondary to that objective. It is possible to desperately desire coolness and attractiveness that one forfeits their desire for Jesus. It is completely possible to be so consumed with being intellectual that we cast faith by the wayside to coincide with our non-Christian intellectual peers that see faith as naivety and ignorance. And probably the most common one, the desire to be loved in a marital relationship can cause us to no longer see a need for God.

All because someone rejected us all those years ago and told us that who we are, as we are, was not enough. And that we needed to do something to be of equal standing with the rest of the world, or at least the world we want to be a part of. The worst part of rejection is that it often leads to self-rejection. People may not be rejecting us anymore, but we reject ourselves for those parts that we think are responsible for putting us in poor standing with our peers or family members. But God has never rejected us for such things, and He never means for us to disqualify ourselves for such things. The truth that we often fail to consider is that we will all experience rejection in our life. It's unavoidable. Even when you do everything right, somebody will disprove. Jesus was rejected. The one and only perfect human being, was rejected and still is today. So what hope do we have? But to change ourselves according to the rejection we've experienced doesn't change that we will be rejected.

Again, rejection can make us completely reorient our lives in search of the elements we believe will make us measure up in our own minds against a standard that was not ours to begin with.

Of course there are more emotions that can derail us, but these are what I would consider to be the riskiest. As well as disillusionment, which I have addressed extensively in my previous book.

Moving Forward

So how do we manage emotions? In truth, for some reading this you may need to consult a counsellor or psychologist. Especially if you already have some trauma and mental health challenges. I'm going to share some basic steps, but you may need someone to work through each step with you. But at the very least this may provide some kind of framework.

1. **Don't deny how you feel**

    Despite what we have been told, feelings are not really controlled by the mind. Well, that would be an oversimplification. No matter what you think, or tell yourself, some emotions will not recede simply because they are unwanted or corrected. I'll discuss more in the following steps, but the point of this first step is to say that our acceptance of where we are emotionally paves the way toward healing. We must recognise the function of denial, because it often prevents us from all that God has for us. Denial is a sign of emotional vulnerability in that it functions to protect us from knowledge and information that our psyche believes we aren't capable of handling. There are times in our life where this is necessary, for instance where a traumatic situation is too severe for us to deal with. Or when we are too emotionally immature or insecure to handle criticism. But in the long run, it simply provides a wall between us and emotional growth. The biggest reason we deny our emotions is because of their unpleasant nature. They don't feel nice. But we are only delaying the inevitable when we simply avoid the emotions we don't like. Because avoidance doesn't diminish them, and dormant emotions have an accumulative nature.

2. **Establish a battle plan**

It isn't normal practice for people to sit down and write a strategy when they are feeling down and I'm not necessarily suggesting something so structured. But there are some basic decisions you can make that will help you in the healing process. For instance, when a friend of mine went through a really difficult time at the outset she made a decision not to drink alcohol. She just didn't want to have any temptations to rely on any kind of substance to get her through, because she knew that it would be hard not to with how difficult the time was to be. For you it might be other things, but at the very least the following are a suggestion of a few helpful decisions to make:

a) **Ensure you have a support network to engage with regularly**

Not only is it critical to have a trusted group of people that can check-in on you, but you also want to let them know that you are going through something so they know to be alert to your needs. Especially if they don't hear from you for a while, it can trigger them to reach out. Remain contactable, no matter how hard it gets. A support network is of no benefit if you aren't contactable.

b) **Initiate prayer support**

Besides praying for yourself, it is good to enlist several people to pray for you. Sometimes when you are going through something hard you can feel as though God isn't there or that God is silent. It can discourage you in your prayer life. As much as you possibly can, keep praying. But if you have a group of people praying for you, not only is it helpful in inviting God into the situation, it also gives an opportunity for others to be a part of God's testimony of faithfulness to you.

c) **Decide to give yourself grace**

Recently, I gave myself grace to pass on social events that I wasn't enthusiastic about. In 2020 I went through a debilitating choking phobia, in which I was unable to consume food for 3 months. During that time, I gave myself permission not to see some people who I knew would be a trigger. This was just to give myself some space to heal. When you have so much going on, you don't need to put pressure on yourself to continue in life as you ordinarily would.

To handle emotions, you are essentially attempting to process them which requires some time and space. You might feel like you don't have that, but sometimes you don't get a choice. But also, the time you take to deal with these emotions will not be longer than the time it would take to get rid of the deep bitterness and resentment you could have because you didn't initially process them. Sometimes when you are in a position of leadership, it can be a lot harder to have time and space. It seems impossible to adjust because everybody expects you to keep doing everything you are. But having people we are responsible for should motivate us even more so to create time and space, for the healing that is to come. Not only will it allow you to continue leading them, but it will also make you a better leader. So, find a way to make some time and space and to give yourself grace.

d) **Process it**

This is the end goal. It's the reason we don't deny our feelings, and it's the reason we establish a battle plan. The processing phase can be very painful, as you discover lies and beliefs that have been lying dormant in your heart now brought to the surface.

The key in this phase is not to run from the emotions, but to prayerfully reflect and attempt to understand them. You may, understandably, need some help with this.

Interestingly, sometimes we know exactly why we are emotionally distraught. When a friend was gossiping about me, I knew exactly why I felt down. But still, instead of just trying to push through I sat in that place of sadness and expressed that hurt to God. The next day I felt almost 100%. I still processed the disappointment with my husband and a close friend, but the intense emotion I felt at first did not have the power over me that it would have if I had just tried to 'move on'. And to this day, I believe that I did not 'sin in my anger' or the other emotions I experienced. The fact is, for those circumstances where we don't understand, there is a prospect of 'renewing our mind'. Because it's likely that what gets us to this place, is an inconsistent or conflicting belief system that requires some change. Facing difficult emotions leads us toward real progress. I recently was struggling with the motivation to write. I proceeded to google all the ways to increase your motivation. It wasn't until a friend said to me that they believe that there may be a deeper cause to my lack of motivation, that I paused to reconsider my situation. She was absolutely right! There were some underlying feelings that I hadn't been acknowledging. Once I started facing those feelings, the path of writing became clearer, and I was able to move forward without simply forcing myself to get on with it.

Every difficult emotion is an opportunity to learn what is going on deeper in our hearts. Every opportunity to understand our hearts is a chance to be cleansed and purified and improve our relationship with God by gaining a clearer vision of Him. Difficult emotions only are truly difficult when they cause us to question and consider disobeying the will of God, which can happen and does happen. For that reason we must learn better ways to manage our emotions, instead of just allowing our emotions to completely take the lead or treating them with condemnation and judgement. Accept your emotions whether they are good or bad, equip yourself to deal with them and then follow God's lead to face them. As painful as it may be, you will thank God for the person you will become for having faced your emotions.

Chapter 8

Unconditional Love

An experienced lobster diver jumps into the water for his second forage for the day. Having already caught 100 pounds of lobster on this average June day in 2021, Michael Packard couldn't have had any reason to think that he would live to tell a story that mimicked a five-thousand-year-old narrative. Possibly accidentally, a humpback whale opened his massive mouth only to gulp Michael down whole! For approximately 45 seconds Michael could feel the whale shaking his head, and finally, he was expelled out of the beast's mouth back to the light of day.[9]

News of Michael Packard's tale spread far, earning him an interview on the well-known American Tonight Show, Jimmy Kimmel.[10]

Besides validating a biblical story, the events of that day demonstrate a belief that has been written about and discussed for some time; humans have a fascination with whales. Truly, the fascination extends to most

---

[9] Fraser 2021
[10] Watch the interview at https://www.youtube.com/watch?v=K7iAlZzVenU

marine life. But whales arouse curiosity and intrigue, with their graceful movement and profound sonar-based communication.

From being the subject of the greatest American novel ever published in Moby Dick to the multitude of documentaries, whales capture and enchant us.

It's really no surprise that of all biblical stories, the story of Jonah and the whale has also enthralled Sunday School children for generations. Though the whale provides the most memorable hook, the lesson preached from this story is as follows: that we must obey God at all costs. The assumption is that if we obey God, we won't get swallowed by a whale. A riveting and true conclusion, yet not necessarily the only conclusion worth drawing. It's not every day that we are asked to do something that could redeem an entire nation, like Jonah. And yet God extended mercy toward Jonah whose response to run was riddled with bad intentions. And whilst Jonah's repentance occurred in the heart of the mammal, we could not so absolutely call the whale God's instrument of judgement, as much as an instrument of mercy. Yes, being in the mouth of a whale would have been a terrifying experience. But it was the men on the ship that tossed Jonah into the waters, assuring his death. The whale prevented his death, providing him with protection for those three days. If anything, it is a reminder that God's mercy is often facilitated in the most unusual of ways. Similarly, when someone gets made redundant from a job they loved, to discover a calling they would never have considered before. Or when a friendship that we didn't recognise was damaging us, comes to an end allowing us to develop new healthy friendships. Or when we lose a significant amount of money on a bad investment only to realise that we had been overestimating how much peace financial security could really give us. The entire story of Jonah demonstrates this ongoing theme of mercy:

1. from God giving the Ninevites a chance.
2. to the whale capturing Jonah.

3. to the moment of lament at the end of the story when God provides shade through a plant.
4. and finally when God teaches Jonah about His mercy rather than chastise him.

God's mercy is steeped throughout this story.

Let's be clear about something: God does not need us. He is quite capable on His own. He also can find others to do His will when we aren't responsive to His call. But God was particularly persistent with Jonah. We don't really know why. But for whatever reason Jonah did not believe Nineveh was worthy of God's mercy - forgetting that no one, including Jonah, is worthy of God's mercy. Yet God was only satisfied with him as His vehicle for deliverance.

Mercy is really an incredible notion. The idea that we undeservedly receive good things from our God is preposterous. Not just that we are pardoned and excused for the sin we commit, but that God could extend blessing upon us too…it's actually quite absurd. So why would God do this? Why would this God who does not need us and gains nothing from us, extend blessing, advantage, honour, and favour to a people who are notoriously inconsistent in their acknowledgement of Him? Why did God offer mercy to the barbaric Ninevites who most likely weren't asking for it? And why was God so merciful to Jonah when he could have just moved on to another prophet to expedite His will? Similarly, why does He persist with us, even offering us grace and mercy when we are ignorant of His ways? There is one reason and no other - LOVE. God's love is so rich, pure and perfect that it is able to give in spite of what He receives, to hope for us despite our obvious failings, to forgive us though He knows we will repent again and again.

1 John 4:8 reads that *"God is love"*. Could there be a more profound statement? What might this statement mean when we consider the great Almighty? To say that He is love is to recognise that all of His actions ultimately emanate out of this pure self-sacrificing love. To have created us and this world would have largely been an act of love. To have given Adam and Eve the choice to eat the fruit from the tree of good and evil, regardless of the grand scale impact of their choice, would have been derived from love. To ask Abraham to sacrifice his son without any intention of letting him follow through, is somehow related to His love. The deliverance in Egypt was rooted in love. God persistently choosing Jonah as His man for the hour, was motivated by love. We could continue in this fashion, noting the various plots in scriptures demonstrating how love motivated such happenings, right up until the climax in the biblical narrative of our Messiah dying upon a cross. But the bottom line is that God is so inherently loving that we cannot separate anything that has been said or done from His loving nature. At the core and centre of God's very being, we find love.

Unconditional Love

I have often wondered whether unconditional love is really possible, especially between humans. In every relationship that exists - parental, child, spouse, sibling, and friendship - we know precisely the actions and behaviours that would nullify all future love and intimacy. If we wanted to, if we were so inclined, we could very quickly lose friends and repel people. For this reason, it can be difficult to comprehend that God could unconditionally love us, especially when we have been brought up to believe that God adopts a consistent stance of readiness to reprimand us, holding a microscope over us waiting for any and all indiscretions. How is He able to love us unconditionally? Do we even really believe that He does?

The scriptures tell us in so many ways that God's love is unconditional. Consider the following verses:

- **Romans 5:8**
  God shows his love for us in that while we were still sinners, Christ died for us.

- **John 3:16**
  For God so loved the world, that he gave his only Son, that whoever believes in him should not perish but have eternal life.

- **Jeremiah 31:3**
  The Lord appeared to us in the past, saying: "I have loved you with an everlasting love; I have drawn you with unfailing kindness. NIV

- **John 15:13**
  Greater love has no one than this: to lay down one's life for one's friends.

And there are more! There are two passages in particular that require deeper consideration. Firstly, Matthew 5:43-48.

> *"You have heard that it was said, 'You shall love your neighbour and hate your enemy.' But I say to you, Love your enemies and pray for those who persecute you, so that you may be sons of your Father who is in heaven. For he makes his sun rise on the evil and on the good and sends rain on the just and on the unjust. For if you love those who love you, what reward do you*

have? Do not even the tax collectors do the same? And if you greet only your brothers, what more are you doing than others? Do not even the Gentiles do the same? You therefore must be perfect, as your heavenly Father is perfect.

In this passage, Jesus describes our heavenly Father as perfect. He is able to love and bless those who are evil and unjust. That means that the worst person you could possibly think of - God loves and blesses. Though God himself would be justified in hating those who bring His name and image into disrepute, He loves and brings good into their lives even though they may never thank Him or acknowledge His involvement. Is this not unconditional love? Furthermore, He encourages us to love in the same manner suggesting that this is the emblem of our sonship. In some ways, Jesus is almost saying that our love isn't really godly unless it can be directed to those who we would naturally be tempted to hate.

Secondly, 1 Corinthians 13:4-8.

Love is patient and kind; love does not envy or boast; it is not arrogant or rude. It does not insist on its own way; it is not irritable or resentful; it does not rejoice at wrongdoing, but rejoices with the truth. Love bears all things, believes all things, hopes all things, endures all things.

Love never ends.

This passage describes a completely self-sacrificing kind of love. A love that has no agenda, that has no intention for personal gain. Furthermore, it describes love as never-ending, not keeping a record of wrongs and enduring all things. Though it may not say 'unconditional' as an explicit quality, this by very nature is a description of love without conditions.

At the very least, we can be confident that biblically God's love is without condition. But how then do we reconcile some of the things we read in scripture? How do we reconcile that hell exists? Or that He is often speaking of punishment and judgement? Are these not opposing ideas?

This is where believers' comprehension of God's love comes undone. When we struggle to reconcile these ideas that we interpret as fundamentally in opposition with each other. Either we are unconditionally loved, or we are conditionally loved with the prospect of punishment and judgement. When we zone in on a specific subject, we can become so narrow-minded that we fail to see that which sits outside of the topic. The fact is, God's love is indeed unconditional. But His forgiveness is not. His forgiveness cannot be unconditional as it would consequently invalidate His perfect justice. Forgiveness is precipitated upon genuine repentance and acceptance of Christ's offer of salvation through His death and resurrection. There is simply no other way. This does not change that God loves us all unconditionally. He loves us entirely whether we are being 'good' or 'bad'. Our qualities do not determine the nature of His love. It is unchanging. Punishment and judgement are therefore dependent on our status of forgiveness. Sometimes the trouble is the discomfort we feel with the word's 'punishment' and 'judgement'. Yes, to be fair, they do appear to be very harsh words. But punishment is merely the consequence of being unforgiven. And judgement is merely the declaration of our status; forgiven or unforgiven. The consequences of this declaration are inevitably harsh, but sin does demand a high cost. It required the arduous death and resurrection of our saviour. When we understand the significance of the cost demanded by sin, we understand the weightiness of forgiveness. But this does not negate the weightiness of God's love either. That Jesus, the Father's very own son, was willing to put his soul, mind and body through the kind of punishment that our sin should attract, entirely for our benefit demonstrates just how loving the Godhead is toward His creation.

When we speak of unconditional love, we speak of the following:

a) **An incomprehensible grace**

We were never made for rejection. If we look to the Holy Trinity, we see that the God-head displays perfect inclusion as an outpouring of mutual love. We, therefore, also were never made for rejection. We were made to bear the image of our creator whose predominant trait is love expressed in mutual inclusivity. That is why rejection is one of the most catalytic events we can personally experience. All of us can identify the points in our own stories when rejection led us down a different path. Maybe toward unhealthy relationships. Or the desire for significance through wealth and power. Or just the desire for safety and security, through comfortable living circumstances.

This inclusivity was something we were unable to be guaranteed by God before Christ paid our debt. Now, therefore, the cross represents an eradication of rejection. To be fair, we can still experience much rejection within our human-to-human relationships. But God alone, because of the grace He has given us promises that nothing will ever have Him reject us when we have received His forgiveness. Especially not the sin that He died to forgive. So no matter where you are in your faith journey, and though you may have some way to go (just like me!) God promises perfect inclusion through His grace. Now, this is an incomprehensible kind of grace! God Himself honours our receptivity with the silencing of sin. There is no limitation on His ability to love and extend grace to us.

b) **The absence of punishment**

Not only does He silence sin, but He also silences any punishable impact our sin once had on us. We are no longer condemned. We receive as a son or daughter would receive. Most astonishingly, we live forever. Our destiny is no longer complete annihilation, the ultimate consequence of sin. Whilst we may experience a physical death it is simply passing from this earthly realm. It does not cease our existence.

c) **Relationship with the Almighty**

And finally, His unconditional love speaks of the privilege to commune and experience our Father relationally. To know His love intimately and share ourselves fully with Him, without fear of judgement or punishment, despite our sinfulness. This is by far the safest relationship we stand to encounter. In this relationship with Christ, we experience a God that is:

- Fully vulnerable and transparent before us. Christ hides nothing. Not even on the cross when He was stripped of His very clothing for our sake. How many relationships can we truly describe this way?
- Severely compassionate. The truth is we would probably consider God a pushover were He living amongst us today as a human. He lavishly bestows mercy and kindness immediately upon our repentance.
- He promises not to harm us and can faithfully deliver on that promise. Yes, we may go through some trials, but none of these is for our harm. If we trust Him through these challenges, we emerge as greater and better functioning disciples than we could have ever been before.

- Perfectly patient and gentle when guiding and leading us. Have you ever stopped to consider how patient God is with you? Sometimes He must teach us the same lesson over and over again. But He never tires, just like a daddy who keeps picking up his toddler trying to learn how to walk. He patiently leads and guides us.
- He does not exclude us or hold us at arm's length. There will never be anything that would cause God to keep you at a distance. I've heard preachers tell believers that they can lose the favour of God. Well, I don't know if that is exactly true, but we certainly didn't see that happen in the story of Jonah. Through shame and guilt, we assume there is a distance. But if only we were to continue to have the audacity to keep walking into the arms of God, we would find that He doesn't exclude us because of the sin we see in ourselves. The fact is, He receives us even with the sin we don't see.
- Always available when we need Him, and always present in every circumstance. There might only be one or two people in my life that would answer my phone call close to every time I call and be available to me. And one of those would be my mother. But it still wouldn't be 100% of the time. My mum for instance is notorious for having left her phone at home, or sometimes she has a nap. Or maybe she doesn't really pay proper attention on the phone, like when she is playing Sudoku on her iPad.

There is no one that is as available to us as God is. The truth is, I've been talking to God in my head for as long as I can remember. I've been talking to Him since before I recognised Him as Jesus. Before I had an image of a God I could understand. That is how accessible He is. Every moment, on any day, for as long as I want...I have the audience of the King. He also promises that He will pay attention, that He will listen, and that every nonsensical, conversational, casual utterance I make is noted and acknowledged by Him. I can't even begin to tell you the number of occasions that I prayed something in passing without my own full consciousness, that He still answered.

And He is present! I am literally never alone. He hears my thoughts, He knows when I wake, and He knows when I go to sleep. Every mundane task and activity I do is accompanied by the Spirit of God.

This is a deep kind of love that we ought to meditate on regularly because it has the power to rattle us out of our comfortable faith.

What does all of this have to do with resilience?

> *Or do you presume on the riches of his kindness and forbearance and patience,* **not knowing that God's kindness is meant to lead you to repentance?**
> Romans 2:4

God is good. God is kind. He is all-loving. These truths change us. They are meant to change us. But they are also the truths that sustain us. It is arguable that there is no other factor more significant than this one when it comes to sustaining a genuine relationship with God.

The fact is, there may not be a better reason than this to sustain our faith in the situations we may find ourselves in. Why would we choose

God over the immediate pleasure that pornography or lust might bring? Because we are profoundly struck by this love, infinitely more significant than any form of pleasure available to us. Why would we choose God over riches, wealth and the pursuits of our worldly brothers and sisters? Because we can't forget what His love has done for us. Not when we know that this love has made us His very children sharing with Him the richness of His blessings, as one of His own. Why would we endure betrayal, why would we forgive our enemies as He instructs us to? Because this love has rattled us so deeply that we cannot bear to hold a debt over another when He has freed us from ours.

It is His love that motivates change. It's His kindness that inspires repentance. We cannot do life without a deeper acknowledgement of God's love. Our very faith is contingent on our understanding of this unconditional love. It is possible that the degree to which our faith is deep is only the degree to which we have comprehended this love. This one note: there are plenty of Christians that roam around every day, preaching a message of standing firm against the culture of this day. They seem like the ones who are steadfast, but they often aren't motivated by love. In fact, they condemn. They put their own righteousness on a pedestal and the message of Christ is far from their lips. I do not call this a deep faith. I call it religious behaviour. Their faith is not in God, their faith is in their religious actions. But for the one who is able to extend love unconditionally to those who seem unlovable, they have begun to understand the depths of God's unconditional love.

When I am searching for the believers who are genuine and mature in their faith, I don't look for the ones who know the most scripture. Or the ones who profoundly declare God's goodness on stage. Or do the longest volunteer hours. I look for the one who can love the person that everyone ignores. I look for the believer who has sinful friends that they aren't embarrassed by. I look for the believer who is patient with the complainer. I look for the ones who can love those who we all struggle to love, and they love without any agenda. Sometimes Pastors don't even fall into this category. They often love people because they want that person to be on a team, to start tithing, or to do some kind of desired activity that they believe is necessary. But unconditional love is without any agenda, nor does it *'insist on its own way'* just as 1 Corinthians 13 referenced earlier demonstrated.

This is our calling. No matter how rough this earth and its inhabitants get, we are meant to extend the kind of love that God extends to us. It is the most critical reason we are here on this earth: to display the love of Christ. Not to build big churches, with the concert-style worship sessions. Not to build a career and earn lots of money. Sure you can go ahead and do those things, but it will never compare to our greatest and most significant personal calling to LOVE OUR NEIGHBOUR. But it is near impossible to love anyone, including yourself if you don't understand the unconditional love that God has for you. Individually and personally. And be able to respond back with this unconditional love to God with our heart, soul and mind. We don't need to fake it. We just need to see His love, in the truest light we can. And allow ourselves to respond according to what we see.

THE Tension

A challenge that Christians often face when it comes to unconditional love is:

1. How do we express this love without condoning someone's ungodly behaviour?
2. How do we balance the tension between loving someone and still truthfully correcting them?

There is this sense that by unconditionally loving someone, they may get the wrong impression. They may incorrectly assume that we condone their behaviour or they may see unconditional love as a free licence to sin as they wish. In my experience, this was a difficult tension to navigate. Until I realised a few significant points, that forced me to take stock of how I was approaching people.

There are some underlying assumptions that we fail to challenge when we ask these questions. Firstly, why would we assume that love condones? When a person participates in criminal activity and is banished for life to jail, do we assume they need more or less love in their life? Do we assume that by withdrawing love that they will come good? There's a good chance that they are in jail, and their participation in all the nefarious activities that got them there, happened because they haven't experienced unconditional love throughout their life. So why would we consider it a risk to love despite a person's behaviour? If I withdraw love when my daughter yells at me, will it change her future decisions to yell? Maybe. But only because of the coldness and rejection she feels from me. Not because she believes the behaviour to be wrong, or that I am worthy of honour as her parent. So which battle do we want to fight? The one that when waged leads to a healthy conviction, that genuinely turns someone from their sin because sin is wrong? Or the war that tells them that they will only receive love when we are doing the 'right thing' according to my interpretation of what is right, that they ought to please man more than God, and further compound this issue of us not comprehending the unconditional nature of love that God expresses to us?

Secondly, the balance between love and truth which I have sarcastically called THE tension. There are actually many tensions in the Christian faith, but I consider this the mother of all tensions. To presume there is a tension between the concepts of love and truth is to assume that on a continuum sits one extreme love and the other extreme truth. That these are the same inherent ideas on a scale, but at odds with each other. Do we believe this to be true? If I were to ask any given Christian what the opposite of love is, they would probably say hate. But there is more reason to believe the opposite to love as God defines it, is a works-based relationship. It's implied in the grammatical construction of the word UNconditional. 'Un' when applied to the word condition, is the opposite. This means that truth isn't even on that scale. I'm not sure what scale truth sits on, but it's not on this one. Inherent in our previously formed continuum, the truth-love scale, is the idea that truth cannot be expressed in love. Or that love cannot be expressed in truth. What a fallacy this is? The scriptures instruct us to speak the truth in love:

> *"Rather, speaking the truth in love, we are to grow up in every way into him who is the head, into Christ"*
> *Ephesians 4:15*

Implied within this statement is that the barrier to truth is not excessive unconditional love, but a truth that is told without unconditional love as its agenda and purpose.

Furthermore, when Jesus told us the greatest of all the commandments in Matthew 22:37-40 he stated:

> *'Love the Lord your God with all your heart and with all your soul and with all your mind.' This is the first and greatest commandment. And the second is like it: 'Love your neighbour as yourself.'* NIV

At no point in this statement did Jesus say, "unless I disapprove of your behaviour'!" The only condition Jesus placed is that this love we express in action and word to our neighbour is at the same degree and level to which we express to ourselves. Some people think this statement means that we can't love others unless we love ourselves. I disagree that this is the overall sentiment of the statement. This statement is more about there being an equal commitment in love to ourselves as to our fellow man. Something very few of us could say we accomplish in this modern world. Either way, Jesus himself is explicit that our responsibility is to love, not necessarily to balance that with the truth. Now there is discernment required here, because of course we are meant to gently guide our brothers and sisters in Christ. But that is not necessarily our concern or priority for the most part.

What these two questions really identify to me, is how deeply we struggle with the concept of unconditional love. To even think that we would be more concerned about condoning behaviour and THE tension over how truly we can express unconditional love, shows how difficult it is for us to receive such love and give it. God does not stop loving us because of our good or ungodly behaviour. God doesn't withhold unconditional love in fear that you might get the wrong message or misunderstand that you still need to change. He just loves us unconditionally, no strings attached, without agenda, without us needing to become righteous or be influential. He loves us in our mess, with our sin, despite our ignorance and despite our rejection of Him. Whatever we would call the opposite of 'cancel culture', is exactly what God is to us. Therefore, when scripture tells us that God is for us, it ought to blow us away. He is infinitely more for us than we are for ourselves.

Final Thought

At some point, we must believe that unconditional love is the only way His Kingdom is established. And if it doesn't make sense how such a love could work, you are on the right track. The Kingdom's values are countercultural, which means that it conflicts with everything we have been taught by this world. Our natural fleshly instinct is to reject such notions. But Jesus set the tone for us, and we are to set the tone for others. God's unconditional love inspired every aspect of the gospel. It is all this world has needed, and it is all we need. If only we could be convinced that unconditional love is our highest priority and pursue its genuine expression in and through us, both toward God and others we would do well to have this gospel in action across the globe.

Chapter 9

Jesus' Resilience

The worst thing about having a shallow faith is the recognition that it is fuelled by a shallow gospel. I know it to be shallow because of what we aren't willing to part with for it. The gospel is such good news that if we were to really grasp it, we would be compelled to gladly abandon all just as so many have done before us. Just like the angels in heaven who, at the very sight of God, are compelled to cry 'holy'. Like Paul who simply had to preach the gospel. Like Jeremiah, who could not stop himself from prophesying. A true vision of God responds in such a way. Something about the gospel we know has been sheltered from our full understanding. And it's not the fault of the gospel, because if the gospel was able to transform anyone it means that it inherently has the capability to transform everyone.

But the same answer is offered to us in our shallow state, as our brothers and sisters in the persecuted church. It's the same textbook Sunday school answer that we ought never to tire of…Jesus. We must consider all He is as the focal point of the Christian faith. In all ways, Jesus provides a model of healthy humanity. He is the one we are to emulate, whilst we simultaneously follow Him. More accurately, to follow Him is to emulate Him. And furthermore, Jesus provides an incredible example of what it means to have a resilient and deep faith. Therefore, to conclude Part 2 let us consider all the ways in which Jesus fulfils these aspects.

The Resilience of Jesus

Unconditional Faith

As you may recall, unconditional faith is the conviction to lay every aspect of our life down in service to Christ, no matter where it takes us. As Jesus prayed on the Mount of Olives, He asked His Father:

> *"Father, if you are willing, remove this cup from me. Nevertheless, not my will, but yours, be done."*
> *Luke 22:42*

He knew what He was to face: an agonising death on a wooden cross. It is likely that having lived around those parts for most of his 33 years, Jesus would have seen others being crucified. He would have seen the condition of their bodies after a full day of torture, the terrifying sound of an anguished soul and the horrendous smell that accompanied a body under distress. He knew what was to come, and He knew that the Pharisees and rulers would have been relentless in ridding this world of a man intent on exposing their corruption. Particularly, one who claimed to have been the 'Messiah' who in their minds should have applauded their pious efforts and taken their side. And so he asked the question of His Father, knowing full well there was no other way. He didn't reason that such an ill-fate could not have been the will of a 'loving' father. He didn't refute such a responsibility as 'not my problem'.

The depth of His love and His righteousness were the very reason he willingly sacrificed himself. True righteousness and perfect love will do that. He gave himself fully to this plan because he had unconditional faith in His Father. He perfectly believed Him and perfectly followed His will.

Just consider the magnitude of this. I once had a job where I was bullied. Everybody told me to leave the job. Now, this may well be the best advice for someone with my own frailties and psychological limits, but Jesus was not deterred by the conditions He would endure. And these conditions included torture so severe that it very nearly could have caused death without the crucifix. Jesus had nothing to ease the physical and mental torture inflicted by the Roman soldiers.

Jesus was motivated by the commitment He had made to the Father. That He would go anywhere, do anything, say anything, in the company of whoever, if it were the Father's will. He had already proved that when He left heaven to resolve a predicament that was technically not His, but ours. And He continued with that commitment right up to and including the cross.

Jesus perfectly demonstrates for us an unconditional faith.

Seek

It is hard to imagine the all-knowing one in need of seeking as we are encouraged to do time and again in scripture. But despite Jesus' nature as both divine and human, he still spent time seeking His Father.

> *"In these days he went out to the mountain to pray, and all night he continued in prayer to God. And when day came,*

he called his disciples and chose from them twelve, whom he named apostles."
Luke 6:12-13

On the flip-side of an all-night prayer session, Jesus chose the disciples. We don't know whether the prayer time was needed as a part of the strategy in deciding upon the disciples. We don't know whether He just needed to mentally prepare himself in the Father's presence to choose Judas, who He knew would betray him to death. All we know is that He prayed ALL NIGHT. Again, it doesn't appear as though Jesus had to do this to commune with His Father. But He did. In fact, He sought out intimacy with His Father every chance He could. More than we would expect a saviour who had already experienced the perfect intimacy of His Father for eternity before his arrival to earth. In fact, maybe that's exactly the point. Maybe that's what made him seek out further intimacy with the Father; it was all he knew, and he knew nothing compared to it. Either way Jesus did not seek His Father because He had to, nor because he was trying to set an example for us though he inadvertently did. He sought His Father because He simply desired to with all His being. I can imagine how eager Jesus must have been to return to His Father, even though He so loved being with the people of God too.

Waiting

If the purpose of Jesus coming to earth was simply to die on the cross, the whole story could have been a lot shorter. No, the fact is that He waited until He was 30 years of age before He even began His ministry and a further three years toward his eventual death and resurrection. We probably underestimate the significance. The Messiah was prophesied about for hundreds of years. Jesus finally comes to earth with intense compassion, yet He would have passed people every day that He could have helped but did not because it was not His time to. There was a matter of timing in terms of when people were to become aware of who He was. He didn't even do his first miracle until He was at a wedding in Cana. And even then, it was through His mother's encouragement. In fact, His very response to his mother was *"My hour has not yet come"* John 2:4. Yet he turned the water into wine, anyway. He had to wait for the moments and times as desired by His Father. Why did Jesus only minister for three years? He could have been ministering, teaching and healing much more than He did. The need was there. Our modern minds naturally gravitate toward maximising the effectiveness of a good thing. We think "how can we have more impact?" But Jesus knew a truth that we sometimes miss these days; the greatest impact we can make is in doing the Father's will, not doing as much as we can. They are not necessarily one and the same thing. Our Jesus is still waiting, as we are, for His return. He tells us that He is busy preparing rooms for us in His Father's house. He is not idly waiting, but the focus of His activity is still in eager anticipation of His eventual return and our entrance.

Jesus doesn't sidestep waiting; He demonstrates perfect patience.

Freedom

It seems impossible that Jesus would ever have experienced any challenges to internal freedom. Afterall, He wasn't bound up by sin like we can be. Nor was He plagued with shame and guilt, besides that which was hauled upon Him when He sacrificed himself on the cross.

But for that reason, He demonstrates the epitome of freedom. For starters, He was not at all concerned with popular opinion. He wasn't even concerned with reputation and credibility. He didn't feel the need to explain or defend His positions, not even when such answers might have freed Him from torture and pain. He simply was not afraid of man.

In an unparalleled act of surrender, Jesus submits himself to the control of the unjust authorities of the day in alignment with the will of His Father. In my generation, there is nothing more terrifying and unjust than someone who takes unwarranted control of another. Our disdain for such abuses is evident in our obsession with gaslighting and anti-power sentiments. We presume that if there is someone with unyielding power, they are likely using that inappropriately and injuring humans on the way to man-made greatness. Jesus on the other hand, knowingly submitted His life into the hands of notoriously corrupt, arrogant, disgustingly powerful entities; both the Romans and the Sanhedrin/Pharisees. Powerful in different ways, no doubt. The Romans wielded power through brute strength and tactical supremacy. They had forced their way into so many cultures and proceeded to rule over them. And the Pharisees and Sadducees ruled in religious and cultural influence. The people relied on them to understand and interpret scriptures so that they might avoid ill health, poverty and ruin at the hand of God. The people were controlled by both these powers. And so Jesus willingly put himself under man-made rule, knowing very well that He was and is the supreme reigning power over all existence. His humility is incomparable. But the point is, you cannot submit yourselves to such control untarnished unless your inner world is completely free. He demonstrates how inner freedom can cause us to endure with peace.

Community

One thing we can be confident of is that Jesus did not hide a single part of himself from His disciples or the people. When He felt moved to cry, He did. When He felt despondent, He grieved. There were no masks that He wore to survive in his community.

But He also demonstrated perfect friendship and continues to do so in His sacrificial love.

He expressed His value of community by instilling community, something that was likely cultural at the time, with the twelve disciples. They were discipled within a community. Even though they had varying degrees of influence in the establishment of the church, He still made community central to their growth as would be for the Early Church.

And of course, Jesus perfectly demonstrates the act of initiation. We must become the kind of community we want to see and experience. Jesus did this when He died on the cross, initiating this global community centred around the gospel. He never exists outside of a community, always united in the Trinity and established as the head of His church.

Managing Emotions

Whilst Jesus displayed many emotions here on earth, none would deter Him from living out His Fathers will. Even when He hurt, even when He was betrayed. He did not pretend His emotions didn't exist, but He also didn't necessarily allow them to rule His actions. When He was arrested unjustly, He did not feel the need to defend His innocence or be validated by man. There is one exception to this. He always allowed compassion to inspire His response to people. He often healed because of compassion. He fed the hungry because of compassion. When He felt compassion, He responded accordingly. Maybe we could argue that compassion is always the Father's will. But it is no doubt an emotion that He took the permission to act upon.

There is another exception that we often are confused about. The day that Jesus cleared out the money lenders in the temple. The scriptures tell us that He overturned tables and seats. John 2 records that He made a whip of cords to drive them out. Most people would interpret this as anger, believing that anger is a sin. And certainly, we are told time and again to be gentle, the apparent opposite of anger. So how do we reconcile this? Did Jesus get carried away in His anger?

Again, anger can be justified. In Mark 3:5 the author notes Jesus' anger when He enters a synagogue on the sabbath and heals a man with a withered hand:

> *"And He looked around at them **with anger**, grieved at their hardness of heart, and said to the man, "Stretch out your hand." He stretched it out, and his hand was restored."*

Jesus was not being ruled by sinful anger. He was experiencing righteous anger, the type that desires to see matters made right. It pleads for restoration and alignment, not punishment and revenge like unrighteous anger would have us do. The expression of His righteous anger was not sin. There was no lasting consequence to His actions to drive out the money lenders and traders.

Unconditional Love

Jesus' own father, Joseph, passed away before His own death on the cross. We know this because Joseph is strangely absent from the narrative after the story where Jesus is teaching in the temple as a child. We also know this because whilst Jesus is dying on the cross, He says for the disciple John to care for Mary, his mother. This tradition would not have been adhered to had Joseph still been alive. We know that Joseph was alive long enough for Jesus to learn His father's trade as a carpenter. But we don't know how long after Joseph's death, that He continued to be a carpenter. Maybe He continued to work for the sake of his family? Maybe He chose not to start His ministry journey until He had adequately provided for His now widowed mother?

It is not uncommon for us to feel as though the world rests on our shoulders. For so many of us, we are simultaneously juggling family responsibilities, financial needs, jobs, friendships, church responsibilities, health concerns, managing a household and even hobbies can sometimes feel like a chore. When I am in an extra busy season, I find myself failing to contact my parents in the usual frequency that I normally do. I don't do it on purpose, it just happens. But Jesus, despite truly carrying the weight of the world on His shoulders, took time to ensure the care of His mother. Had you or I been dangling on a cross in excruciating pain, we would be warranted a little leeway for having been self-focused at the time. But Jesus' compassion stayed ripe as He looked upon His mother honouring her with compassionate love.

Furthermore, as Jesus hung on the cross He asked His father to forgive those responsible for His predicament. Whilst He is facing death, He is concerned about the status of these humans in the sight of God. It is such an odd piece of scripture really if you think about it. They weren't asking Him for forgiveness. Jesus was offering this on their behalf, pre-emptively, knowing that they were unable to have the kind of breadth of understanding for all that was going on. And truly their anger that placed Him on the cross, was somewhat necessary (or maybe less necessary, but rather exactly what God predicted) as this was the death that would free us all. Regardless, we here have another example where Jesus makes another statement from the very crossbeam that is of great benefit to others. It also demonstrates that

He did not hold this action against them. He wasn't seeking vengeance; He wasn't seeking compensation. He had forgiven them and therefore appealed to His father for the same pardon. This is love! All of us will have adequate occasion to forgive. Fewer of us will have the opportunity to forgive like this. Nevertheless, we still struggle with the degree of forgiveness we are required to deal with. Yes, of course, there are big things to forgive. Harm is rampant in this world. The #MeToo movement showed us that there is a regularity of abuse that should make us notably uncomfortable in this world. But again, Jesus demonstrates a kind of forgiveness to aspire to. His forgiveness is motivated by love and compassion, not personal freedom. Often, we hear messages of forgiveness and the primary motivator offered to us is to release ourselves from the harm that unforgiveness brings. But Jesus wasn't motivated by this as we can see in His statement that he was concerned for them:

> *And Jesus said, "Father, forgive them, for they know not what they do." And they cast lots to divide his garments.*
> Luke 23:34

Final Thoughts

Reading the acts of Jesus inevitably makes me wonder "What hope could I possibly have of being like Him?" He is perfect in every way, and we are so imperfect. But that is precisely the reason we have hope. Because the Spirit of the One who could do such things lives in us. The very same Spirit echo's the life and words of Jesus through us if only we allow the Spirit to form and change us and remove all barriers.

JESUS' RESILIENCE

Having a resilient faith is possible because, and only because of the influence of the Holy Spirit. Having an unconditional faith, seeking, waiting, experiencing freedom, experiencing community, managing our emotions well and displaying unconditional love are ways in which we participate with the Holy Spirit in the maturation process. You don't have to look for these opportunities. Because of the Holy Spirits' desire to grow you into Christlikeness, these opportunities will no doubt present themselves every day. The resilience on our behalf is to bounce back from every circumstance and trial by allowing every one of these categories to develop us into greater disciples of Jesus Christ. Every trial and challenge is a chance for us to grow and allow the Holy Spirit to impart a deeper faith within us.

In Part 2, I will discuss two broad areas of change that are a natural progression of the resilient faith we are developing deep within. These chapters will be deliberately briefer but are intended to identify in ourselves how deep our resilience has developed with the intention of going deeper.

PART 2

Chapter 10

Obedience

Obedience is such a significant discussion point in scripture that I must talk about it. But alas, it did not necessarily fit in Part 2 as I had originally planned. Because the truth is, genuine obedience is largely the outcome of deepening faith, rather than a precipitator of one. In the early stages of faith, we obey because that is what God told us to do. Sometimes it is motivated by a fear of falling short of the Christian standard. And sometimes it is motivated by a fear of making a mistake and being 'outside' of the will of God. But when our faith deepens, we obey because we desire it. We obey because we are confronted with all we know about Christ. It is simply the only natural response to His goodness. There is a substantial difference. One can be self-serving, one is a form of worship.

It is a deepening revelation of Christ that transforms self-preservation obedience into worshipful obedience.

In this chapter, I will explore and define the nature of the kind of obedience we see when a deep and resilient faith has become our pursuit. In a way, it gives us a sign of the transformation that is evident within ourselves.

OBEDIENCE

Self-preservation vs Worship

It is necessary to delve into this concept because it promises to keep hidden psychological realities that are detrimental to our obedience to God. When we obey God from a place of worship and adoration, we express value in His opinion and thoughts. We are honouring His voice above our own. We recognise His wisdom over ourselves and our instincts. This is not an easy thing for most humans to do. We are very reliant on our own interpretation and instincts, almost exclusively and are taught to do so.

A couple of years ago, when I was dealing with the choking phobia mentioned earlier, I had this wildly raw revelation. So many of my attempts to obey God were ruled by punishment. I stayed between the lines God had suggested because I was afraid of what might happen to me. It was self-preservation that motivated my actions, which at its core were still, to a significant degree, a self-centred reason to obey. It's possible that we see something like this in the story of the prodigal son, in the life of the brother who remained at home. He was disgruntled with his father's response to his brother. Because he wasn't serving his father out of adoration and love. If he was, he would have understood and empathised with his father's response to the son he thought he had lost forever.

I had to confront the limitations of this belief system. Would I obey Him if there was no personal gain for me? If it didn't preserve me and my interests? Not always. Why had I believed that God was so eager to punish me? I imagined God bent down at the thin line between obedience and disobedience, with his magnifying glass and his measuring tape just waiting to remove his favour the moment I went even a millimetre out of bounds. Does God want me to obey like that? No, He doesn't. I had to recognise that I was afraid of God and the power He had to take from me what I really wanted. I was afraid of God, more than I loved Him. Of course, I have spent time working through this with God, and for the most part, I now endeavour to obey Him because I love, worship and adore him. This is what it means to value His voice.

Radical

A deep faith leaves you less concerned with your former worries and motivations. I'm still growing, but I am no longer concerned whether I am a success as defined by the world. I can't even explain how factors that once influenced my every waking activity, are no longer important or even interesting. This makes me comfortable and content to do only what I believe God is directing me to, regardless of what I personally gain in credibility for it. I consider that completely radical for who I once was. And I would say many other believers would find this strange too, having grown up in the same society that drums worldly success into us.

But as we pursue depth, it is normal for priorities to change. Motivators that were important to us, become less so. It gives us room to naturally become even more radical in our obedience. John the Baptist was unlikely to have become a locust eating, desert dweller overnight. It would have been revelation after revelation that continued to grow him deeper into the man that was willing to give up his very reputation for his renewal movement. Depth will inevitably lead to radical obedience. That may scare you. But that is the obedience that is required. We ought to heed to the words of Revelations 12:11

> "They triumphed over him by the blood of the Lamb and by the word of their testimony; **they did not love their lives so much as to shrink from death.**"

To not love our lives, or not shrink from death requires a level of radical obedience that is uncommon in our modern world. There is something a person capable of this understands about life and death that motivates them to respond like this to persecution. There is a perspective that they have that is convinced that comfort in this life is not nearly as valuable as we think. That is radical! And that is what we develop naturally, by pursuing depth in our relationship with Christ.

Listening

The number of times I have heard Christians say "The Bible is clear" on a particular topic, only to realise that they have taken the words at face value without ever considering the context and times in which the passage was written? Too many to count.

I admit I don't love talking about the Bible from an intellectual and theological perspective with everyone. I sometimes feel like in the Christian world there is an invisible hierarchy that is ascertained based on your apparent knowledge of scripture. And in my experience, it is not necessarily the knowledgeable that are willing to live out scripture with abandonment. Many just like talking about it. I can be easily drawn into intellectual discussions because of my inquisitive mind. But I don't ever want to fall into the temptation of thinking that my faith is measured in understanding and not in action. I once mentioned to a previous Pastor that I wanted to go deeper in our Small Group gatherings, and he automatically (as so many would) assumed that I wanted to get into more theological discussions around scripture. That is not at all what I meant. And it's not at all what I am trying to relay to you, the reader, throughout this book. Hopefully you can see that my commitment is to an improved Orthopraxy. As opposed to Orthodoxy, meaning right doctrine and belief, Orthopraxy refers to right behaviour or actions. Correct Orthodoxy is of course critical to the life of a believer. But Orthopraxy is doctrine in practice. Do we live up to what we believe? Are we more committed to this than anything else?

However, when we are committing to a deepening of our faith, simply accepting a surface level interpretation of scripture just won't do. We begin to realise that scripture is very rarely straightforward, and how could we really presume it to be? It is a collection of many books written by multiple authors, with different themes, written more than 2000 years ago, in a completely different culture with almost diametrically opposing values…in completely different languages. Some of which are more accurately termed ancient languages. The original Hebrew scriptures didn't even have vowels. A deepening faith, because of its natural desire to be resolutely obedient, naturally increases our dedication to listening to God. And our listening skills are only enhanced by grappling with scripture and pushing deeper into what God is saying, and not only what we are reading of our own understanding into scripture. Listening is a key aspect of obedience. Jesus so often says:

> "Whoever has ears to hear, let him hear"
> Mark 4:9

It is not only suggesting that everyone should listen. It is also saying that our obedience and ability to follow Jesus is reliant on us listening well. My daughter is pretty bright, but she can get overwhelmed at times. When she is in that state, to be able to help her navigate her through I must listen as much to what she is not saying as what she is. Because her articulation is not perfect in those moments. Listening is my greatest asset at those times.

Becoming a more obedient believer, means we will want to listen more attentively to what God might be saying that we weren't willing to hear before.

Walking Alone

When we begin to be radically obedient, there is a good chance we will have seasons where we have had to abandon the path walked by many of our peers for the sake of our God. Or we will walk a path that doesn't appear to be the logical next step. That's because God will often test our dedication to Him alone, and not the prescribed model that we have seen the majority walk out. It is unlikely that all of our paths of obedience are the quintessential models: study, get married, buy a house, have kids. A model that is seen often. That doesn't mean it isn't God's will if this is exactly how it has happened for you. But there is a good chance that God's plan of obedience is not going to be the same for most believers. Because He has unique callings for all of us, and so it would be at least somewhat safe to assume that our paths will also differ. It may not be everybody's path to buy a house. That's a struggle for Christians to consider, because there is such societal pressure both from outside and within the church that presumes home ownership. It won't be God's will for every person to be married. It can't be! It won't be God's will that every person has children, or that every person has children before their 40's. It was God's will for Abraham and Sarah to have a child in old age, so why would it be God's will that all of us have all our children in our 20's.

It is important to understand this, because obedience may not look right to those around you and you will have to walk a lonely path for a season. You may be the only one doing what you are doing, with your specific lifestyle. Yes, it will be lonely, and others won't understand. But

God will and He knows what He is doing. Even in Matthew 16, when Jesus is explaining to the disciples that He will be killed and raised to life in three days, Peter is unable to fathom that this could be God's will. And He refuses Jesus' statement. But Jesus rebukes this saying:

> "Get behind me, Satan! You are a stumbling block to me; you do not have in mind the concerns of God, but merely human concerns." NIV

The truth is, like Jesus has stated here, our peers don't always understand what God has in store for us. They often respond with human concerns clouding their judgement. At some point our obedience will lead us to walk a path that they won't agree with, and that might just mean you are deepening your faith.

Final Thoughts

In Exodus 33:15 Moses and God have been discussing the clarity Moses is needing in leading the people of God. He says this astounding comment:

> "If your Presence does not go with us, do not send us up from here." NIV

When you begin to really deepen your faith, and obedience naturally flows from your life and witness…this verse holds the sentiment of how you feel. It's not about where you travel or where you find yourself, as long as the presence of God is with you. As long as it is where He has led you. The fact is, we will have hardship wherever we go. Even if we land our dream job, in our dream location, with our dream spouse and our dream kids. Hardship is a given. And so is blessing! And the inverse of this is true also. Even if you land the worst job, in the crummiest area, with issues in your marriage and difficult kids. There will be hard days as well as seasons of blessing. Because *the rain pours on the just and the unjust* (Matthew 5:45). Which means that the circumstances don't define for you the rightness of your path, it's whether God's presence led you here, stays with you there. That becomes the most important matter, for those who are developing the kind of obedience borne of a resilient faith.

Chapter 11

Service

Service is a virtue of the Christian faith. When we love God, we will serve Him and our fellow humans. Usually in the capacity that we are most gifted in. But when deepening really begins to occur, service becomes something we must do and be willing to step out of our comfort zone. Leading us to do what must be done, and not necessarily what we take pleasure in. That in itself is hard for modern day believers to comprehend. Service when you have a resilient faith, is needs-based not satisfaction-based. I'll be the first to admit that I am not close to being a believer who serves without desiring personal satisfaction. But I know what I am aiming for. I did a job that I didn't really like, and I complained to God and threatened to quit every day. Now I know that most modern Christians aren't living needs-based-service, because the hardest ministries to serve in are always notoriously understaffed, and under-volunteered. So, we could stand to grow in this area as a whole. But again, maybe that is more of a testament to the urgency in growing in our depth and resilience…the overall theme of this book.

SERVICE

So let me clarify and define 'serving':

- Anything that is intended to bring glory to God and Him alone.
- Anything we do that is intended to express the value of man as seen by God and provide accordingly.

This means that service is not for our personal gain. To serve in this manner, would be called selfish ambition which scripture vehemently opposes:

> *"Do nothing out of selfish ambition or vain conceit. Rather, in humility value others above yourselves"*
> *Philippians 2:3*

It is inevitable that service at times will benefit us, but this isn't supposed to be a motivating factor. In the past, I have failed miserably and demonstrated to myself that my serving was 'self-serving'. For many Christians, serving can be a way of experiencing approval and relational value. But at the core of it, such serving is not really serving. Now maybe we ought to take this principle Paul discusses in Philippians 1:15-18 regarding preaching the gospel:

> *"It is true that some preach Christ out of envy and rivalry, but others out of goodwill. The latter do so out of love, knowing that I am put here for the defence of the gospel. The former preach Christ out of selfish ambition, not sincerely, supposing that they can stir up trouble for me while I am in chains. But what does it matter? The important thing is that in every way, whether from false motives or true, Christ is preached." NIV*

Yes, it is true that our motivation for serving probably makes little difference to the recipient. Either way, they will receive the intended blessing. The only exception to that is when your service is in an influential leadership position: if service is motivated by anything self-centred it will likely end with harm to others. But, yes, for the most part, putting flyers on the church seats so that the good-looking service leader notices you, is probably not going to make any difference to the person who sits in that space. But it will make a difference to you! We are the ones who are negatively affected by service that is not inspired by our love for God and His people. Because, for that, we don't reap any reward in heaven. We won't grow in our approval addiction if we keep feeding it, instead of healing it through the power of the Holy Spirit.

Now, none of this means we ought to wait until we are holy and complete before we start serving. None of us would serve if this were so. Quite simply, be aware of the goal. When we develop a resilient deep faith, we will come to serve because of God's glory and the value of people.

Your Vision Will Get Broader

Previously, as a church leader, all my service went to my church. The people of God were my muses. I created programs for them, I innovated for them, I responded to their frustrations. They were my inspiration. Unfortunately, in at least one of the seasons, I forgot about my family. If my family asked me for something I would feel like it was a hassle, and that I was the victim. When I stopped volunteering at that church, I saw the way in which my relationships with my family had declined. I am one of the only nieces in my family. Which means all my Aunties see me as another kind of daughter. And I love that. I have taken trips overseas with my Aunties, with me organising the taxi's, paperwork, and luggage. I once took my Aunty on a trip around the USA, on my travel discount - I was working for an airline at the time - and we had a sensational time. So I really regretted how I had allowed those relationships to take a back seat.

When I resigned from my position on staff at my last church, I realised that there was so much service that happens in a church that is not considered official 'serving'. There was a lady I knew who met up every day for coffee with ex-pastors and leaders, praying and prophesying. I remember having a dream in that year of stepping down that showed her as the Worship Pastor of our church. I remembered waking up thinking: "She is the worship leader! She shows people every day how to worship God by loving the people who have been forgotten". She still texts me almost four years later. Her service doesn't improve our volunteer statistics. But it is more valuable than many rostered volunteer roles. When we start to build a resilient and deep faith, our vision isn't limited to what church leadership tells us is available. We will see needs everywhere and seek to serve. We will cross cultural borders to serve. Like the Good Samaritan who took no notice of the cultural ramifications of his service. This is because when we deepen our faith, our compassion grows. And when our compassion grows, the barriers start coming down.

Final Thoughts

I promised that these chapters would be shorter, but I must admit I even shocked myself in this one. So here is my final thought.

In the Kingdom, service is worship. We serve because we love and adore Him. It is the evidence that our hearts are consumed with wonder at His glorious majesty. It is an act of humility and surrender.

God has served us generously. He provides for us, and even most generously He provided us with a saviour. He ministers. He leads. He heals.

He comforts us. All this He does, for us…still. Giving himself in service is the most natural thing for God to do. And it would stand to reason that it would become our action too, when we are growing deeply into Christlikeness.

Service is the greatest call any of us are given. We tend to think that pastors and missionaries have the greatest call of all, but we have all been given this huge calling when we are told to serve our fellow man. And so I leave with you this reminder:

> *"Whatever you do, work at it with all your heart, as working for the Lord, not for human masters"*
> *Colossians 3:23*

Conclusion

>>>>>——→

Shallow waters are safe. It would be rare to find challenges, rare to face big waves or turbulent waters in the shallow parts of the ocean. Shallow waters are so safe that it is typically where we would allow the most inexperienced of swimmers. They are the easiest waters to exit and we find it easy to enter.

Compare this to Diane Nyad[11] in 2013 a decorated and experienced swimmer who at the age of 64 swam from Cuba to Florida without a shark cage. A 177km (110 miles) swim amongst venomous jellyfish and deadly sharks. Consider Veljko Rogosic[12], another experienced accomplished swimmer, who swam the greatest recorded distance without flippers or a wetsuit, a mammoth 224km (139.8 miles) across the Adriatic Sea. Rogosic was aged 65 at the time, and he accomplished the swim in 50 hours and 10 minutes. What kind of faith must one have in their own swimming ability to conquer such a goal? What kind of faith must one have in their ability to endure and adapt, knowing full well that the sea is an unpredictable adversary bringing many experienced men and women to their death? There is nothing safe about the open seas. There is constant resistance through the sheer force of the tide. There are creatures that lurk beneath willing to

---

[11] *Diana* 2022
[12] Munatones, 2012

attack. Then there is the temperature of the waters, and the wind conditions. And the waves that can tower over ships and vessels like monolithic skyscrapers. It is truly terrifying what the oceans can produce. An open water ocean swim is the riskiest of all swimming events. But anyone who could master the kinds of swims that Nyad and Rogosic conquered, might very well have a chance of conquering any kind of waters.

For most of us, God graces us with gentle faith experiences in our early stages of faith because we are not mature enough to handle anything more. That is not a shameful thing, but a necessity for our survival. But at some point, ease can quickly become dangerous for our faith. Because even if we avoid trials and challenges, they have a way of finding us. Without the ongoing training or experience with this 'open sea' kind of faith, we don't stand much of a chance. Either we are forced to grow exponentially and suddenly. Or we exit the faith.

The fact is the intention has always been to venture to the open seas. The open seas promise challenge, they promise hardship. That is the kind of faith we signed up for when we decided to follow Jesus. We forget that to follow Jesus, is to emulate him. And the truth is His life ended on the cross before He rose again. The same fate awaits us: taking up our cross will inevitably lead us through challenge and hardship. But the person who has journeyed with God and endured, knows that there is greater reward when we die to ourselves, to truly live a renewed life in Christ.

Those times we've wondered whether there is something missing, we were right! Something is missing! We have been trying to scale the depths in shallow water. A redundant activity. We get to the deep experiences of faith: fearlessness, courage, miracles, glory, revival, His continual ministering, His presence, communing with Him face to face…in the open seas. And there is only one way to get to the open seas and survive it. Begin the journey toward deepening our faith.

INTRODUCTION TO PART 1

The same principle applies to us and our faith, as open water adventurists Nyad and Rogosic: if we endure deep enough and far enough in our faith, there will come a point when virtually no challenge can overthrow us. Because we have confidence through the power and presence of the Holy Spirit, to adapt to whatever may come.

A deepening faith is our only option.

Bibliography

Kiver, EP & Harris, DV, 1999, *Geology of US Parklands,* John Wiley & Sons Inc, New York

Szalay, J 2017, *Giant Sequoias and Redwoods: The Largest and Tallest Trees* viewed July 2020 https://www.livescience.com/39461-sequoias-redwood-trees.html

Alpine Nurseries 2021, *Jacaranda Mimosifolia,* viewed January 2022 https://www.alpinenurseries.com.au/jacaranda-mimosifolia/

Chen, H, *Readers ask: What Is The Root System Of A Jacaranda Tree?,* viewed May 2022, https://lastfiascorun.com/interesting/readers-ask-what-is-the-root-system-of-a-jacaranda-tree.html

Nguyen D 2022, *Divorce Rate by Country: The World's 10 Most and Least Divorced Nations in 2022,* Unified Lawyers, viewed July 2021 https://www.unifiedlawyers.com.au/blog/global-divorce-rates-statistics/

Hinton, A & Burke, J 2014, *Tashi And The Monk,* online video, viewed December 2018, <https://www.youtube.com/watch?v=-Y0_-hmvxPM>

Fraser, D 2021, *'I was completely inside': Lobster diver swallowed by humpback whale off Provincetown,* Capecod Times, viewed February 2022, https://www.capecodtimes.com/story/news/2021/06/11/

humpback-whale-catches-michael-packard-lobster-driver-mouth-provincetown-cap-cod/7653838002/

Diana 2022, viewed January 2022, http://diananyad.com/diana/

Munatones, S 2012, *Veljko Rogosic: A Croatian Legend Passes,* World Open Water Swimming Association, viewed January 2022 https://www.opernwaterswimming.com/veljko-rogosic-croation-legen-passes/

Reflection Questions

Introduction

1. What have you noticed about the early church when reading the New Testament?
2. What does having a deep faith mean to you?
3. What is your response to Mel's thoughts about being willing to sacrifice our lives for the gospel? Is she being too harsh?
4. How are your actions demonstrating faith? Would you like that to improve?
5. What are you expecting God to do in your life, through this book?

Chapter 1 - Resilience in Faith

1. What feelings arise when you consider the scripture in Matthew 24:9-10? What is your response to being hated? Persecuted? Betrayed?
2. Do you believe you are ready for the days that Jesus spoke about in Matthew 24?

3. How have you observed a resilience level within your own faith journey? Has your faith in Jesus changed because of certain circumstances you've been through?
4. Do you see trials as an opportunity to grow your character?
5. When you reflect upon your own life how attached are you to it and what are the signs of that attachment?
6. How is your life a dynamic testimony of Christ's incomparable grace? What in your life points to Jesus?
7. What must die in you, for you to truly live?

Chapter 2 - Unconditional Faith

1. Do you think it is possible to love unconditionally? Do you see limits on your own ability to love people without condition?
2. What are some relationships that exist in society where it is socially acceptable for conditions to apply?
3. In what ways has your response to God been conditional?
4. What impact does a transactional relationship have on intimacy?
5. How do you relate to the nature of Jacob's relationship with God on page 19?
6. How might your relationship with God progress if there were to be no conditions in your engagement with Him?
7. How would knowing that you must get through a trial, change how you reacted to those trials?

Chapter 3 Seeking

1. How do you stay in love with God?
2. What have you understood 'seek' to mean in scripture?

REFLECTION QUESTIONS

3. On page 30, Mel makes two comparisons between the believer who has given up the search for God and the believer who engages in deep searching. Which resonates with you the most?
4. How can we as believers resist the temptation to think we know all there is to know about God?
5. Do you use the SOAP method? How might you be able to change how you approach the SOAP method to gain a greater understanding of God?
6. Have you gotten busy and distracted and forgotten that there is still more to God? How could you change this?

Chapter 4 Waiting

1. What have you had to wait for? How rewarding or devastating was the experience?
2. What was the hardest part of the waiting? How did your image of God change during the waiting season? What aspects of faith did you question because of the waiting season?
3. Of the reasons Mel provided in the section titled "Why must we wait" (pages 38-40), which reason seemed the most relevant to your seasons of waiting?
4. What difference does considering the ways in which God has waited, change your perspective on waiting? Is it something you've ever appreciated before?
5. How would you describe the relationship between waiting and hope? How could the hope you have in Jesus reframe your seasons of waiting?

Chapter 5 Freedom

1. Describe a time in which you felt free. What was happening at that time?
2. What have you understood freedom to be? Does it align with biblical freedom?
3. In what ways have you seen religion and religious activity become oppressive?
4. Sin is by far the greatest oppressor we could face and the greatest threat to our freedom. Do you agree or disagree? Why?
5. How could the hope of eternal life help us to face our fears today?
6. What actions and choices have you made from guilt? Or out of shame? In hindsight, were they the right choices?
7. On page 58, Mel provided a list of ways in which we rely on God. Which ones do you struggle with, and which one are you progressing well with?

Chapter 6 Community

1. Do you agree that we underestimate the value of community? What do you see in scripture that validates a community's influence on the person?
2. When have you felt like you didn't identify with a community? What impact did it have on how you contributed to that community?
3. When have you felt like you did identify with a community? What difference did it make to your engagement with that community?
4. Are you ever tempted to fake resilience in faith, in the communities you find yourself in? What would have to change in your community interactions if resilience in faith became your greatest priority?

REFLECTION QUESTIONS

5. What would it mean to be a part of a 'Iron sharpens Iron' community? Does it sound attractive to you? Why or why not?
6. Take an overview of your life. How high a priority is friendship in your own life?

Chapter 7 Managing Emotions

1. What do you tend to struggle with more, denying emotions or being ruled by emotions? Why might that be?
2. What do you think is the purpose of emotions? How might emotions be helpful for us?
3. What emotions do you feel uncomfortable with? (For instance, maybe you feel embarrassed by them, or try to hide them.)
4. What is your relationship with loneliness? How has it impacted your decisions and choices?
5. How about rejection? How has it impacted your choices?
6. Of the four emotions mentioned (loneliness, pain and sorrow, betrayal and rejection) which has been the most impacting on your life choices? Which could pose a threat to your faith, if you were unable to learn how to handle them?
7. What is the greatest barrier to processing your emotions and therefore experiencing healing?

Chapter 8 Unconditional Love

1. Have you always perceived the whale in Jonah's story as a vehicle of mercy? How might the challenges we face be a form of mercy?
2. What does 'God is love' mean for you? What does it mean for your relationship with Him?

3. Do you sometimes wonder whether unconditional love is truly achievable in human to human relationships?
4. In your closest relationships, are you able to love without an agenda?
5. How would you live your life with Christ if you knew there was no punishment?
6. How have you struggled because of 'THE tension'? How has a concern for condoning affected your ability to love unconditionally?
7. Do you struggle to contemplate God's love for you? If so, why? What is it about you that makes you think he would love you less?

Chapter 9 Jesus' Resilience

1. Can you think of other ways in which Jesus demonstrates a resilient faith?
2. Which area presented in this chapter speaks to you the most?
3. What areas would you like to see God at work in? Take a moment to pray and ask God to form a deeper faith in you.
4. How can you rely on the Spirit to see these changes take place in your own life?

Chapter 10 Obedience

1. Do you find it difficult to follow someone's lead? What difference does it make when you trust the person and have a good relationship with them?
2. What is your response to the idea of obedience as a form of self-preservation? Has self-preservation ever underpinned your obedience to God?
3. Are there limits to your ability to obey God? What are they?

REFLECTION QUESTIONS

4. What areas of obedience have you walked out, only to discover it to be a lonely road? Why do you think that is? How hard is it to obey God when others don't understand the path for you?
5. What has God been saying to you throughout this book that has required a deeper kind of listening?

Chapter 11 Service

1. Are there times when service has given you some personal gain? How easy is it for that personal gain to become the purpose of our serving?
2. What kind of service do you find hard to do?
3. What service do you believe God is calling you to do?

Conclusion

1. What are the key areas you have felt God speaking to you about throughout this book?
2. What one prayer could you regularly commit to God for the next few months, to see the turnaround that God is leading you toward?
3. How can you maintain focus and prevent distraction in your efforts to deepen your faith?
4. What specific actions could you take to continue this journey of deepening?

www.ingramcontent.com/pod-product-compliance
Lightning Source LLC
Chambersburg PA
CBHW060529100426
42743CB00009B/1473